The Story of Iona

Rosemary Power is a member of the Iona Community, and has given talks and retreats in Britain and Ireland; and courses on the island of Iona and elsewhere, in particular on the traditional spiritualities of the Celtic world.

She has a doctorate in medieval Norse-Gaelic literature, and has written extensively on the Hebrides in the Middle Ages. She also writes and speaks on folk tradition, and has a research degree in theology.

Her recent books include *The Celtic Quest: A Contemporary Spirituality* (Columba, 2010); and *Sacred Places and Pilgrim Paths: Kilfenora, Killinaboy and Scattery Island* (Columba) is forthcoming. She has a book on the illustrations in the *Book of Kells* to be completed shortly.

The Story of Iona

*Columban and Medieval Sites
and Spirituality*

Rosemary Power

CANTERBURY
PRESS
Norwich

First published in 2013 by the Canterbury Press Norwich
Editorial office
3rd Floor, Invicta House,
108–114 Golden Lane,
London EC1Y 0TG

Canterbury Press is an imprint of Hymns Ancient & Modern Ltd
(a registered charity)
13A Hellesdon Park Road, Norwich,
Norfolk NR6 5DR, UK

www.canterburypress.co.uk

Scripture quotations taken from the Holy Bible, New International
Version © 1973, 1978, 1984 by International Bible Society.
Used by permission of Hodder & Stoughton Ltd, a member of
the Hodder Headline Ltd.

Psalm quotations are from *The Psalms: An Inclusive Language Version
Based on the Grail Translation*, 1993, London: Harper-Collins.

British Library Cataloguing in Publication data

A catalogue record for this book is available
from the British Library

978 1 84825 556 2

Typeset by Regent Typesetting, London
Printed and bound in Great Britain by
Ashford Colour Press, Gosport, Hants

Contents

Acknowledgements

Many people have made the comments that led to the creation and completion of this book. Thanks are due to those who gave ideas and offered interpretations during talks and tours. Special thanks are due to David Coleman, a former Iona abbey guide, for the use of his photographs and for his thoughtful interpretations of the fabric. He, Tony Phelan and David Bunney read and commented on the text, while Zam Walker offered suggestions over many conversations. Janet MacDonald assisted me with the historical background, especially the economics, and allowed me to use her unpublished PhD. Janet Harbison, Sheila Crotty and Anne Crotty showed me how the buildings sound for music and the human voice. Tasha Gefrey allowed me to use her unpublished findings on the high crosses. Thanks are also due to Des Bain for support and the time to complete the book; to Olive Carey, Barbara Mackay, Jenny Meegan and Kay Muhr; to the Historic Scotland site guides for their views; and to the critical support and encouragement of fellow-members of the Iona Community. Any errors are my own.

List of Illustrations

The publisher and author acknowledge with thanks permission to use photographs. Wikimedia Commons images are available under a Creative Commons Attribution-ShareAlike 3.0 licence. Unattributed photographs are by the author.

Map of Iona

Eilean Chalbha
(Calf Island)

Strand of the Seal

White Strand
of the Monks

Well of Eternal Youth

Dun Ì ▲

Bishop's Walk

Hermit's Cell ●

Clachanach ●

†Duke of Argyll's Cross

▲Dun Bhuir

Macleod Centre ●

† IONA ABBEY

Reilig Oran ●

Port Bàn

Parish church ●

Cnoc Mòr ●

†Maclean's Cross

St Ronan's Bay

Hill of the Angels

Nunnery ●

Jetty

Maol ●

Martyrs' Bay

Clachancorrach ●

The Machair

Cnoc Orain ●

Bay at the Back
of the Ocean

Lagnagiogan

Greenbank

Traigh Mhòr

Spouting Cave ●

Sandeels Bay ●

St Martin's
Caves

▲Loch Staoineig

▲
'The hill with its
back to Ireland'

Pigeon's Cave ●

Columba's Bay ●

Marble Quarry

Port of the Coracle

Map of the region

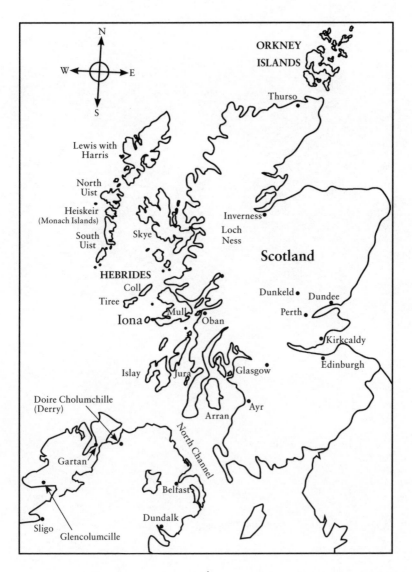

Introduction

Iona is a place of pilgrimage, historical interest and tourism. It has been since the Irish saint Columcille, Columba in Latin, arrived in the sixth century, traditionally in 563 AD. This book seeks to serve the visitors who come to an island where there are physical remains that mark centuries of prayer, and which are important to them today.

It seeks to be a historical guide to the sites, including to some of the lesser-known features, while also identifying a small amount of what we know of how others have experienced the same site in the past.

We are continuing to make the history of Iona. A visitor today comes with their own story and needs, and many find in the richness and depth that pervades the island something that resonates with their own spiritual life. Some come because of the site's historical interest, and many combine this with a search for a deeper understanding of how people lived here before our times, and how Iona became a spiritual centre.

This sense of the spiritual is constantly renewed by what people bring as well as by what they are open to receiving. This book is aimed at those who want some information, to enable them to enter more fully into what makes this historical site a place that touches the deeper experiences of our lives. It is intended as a reflective guide for those who want to linger and sense something of the continuity that makes Iona a distinctive and sometimes life-changing place. It also attempts to show how the island continues to attract layers of interpretation, historical and spiritual, by those who lived here, and by pilgrims who came down the centuries.

The process of seeking to understand the call of the divine in one's own time has gone on ever since Columba first came to this island, and possibly before. There is something extraordinary in the ways in which many visitors today not only receive from the time spent on the island but bring something that serves to make the place continue as a place of safety and energy in which to explore the deeper urges of the human spirit. There is an atmosphere that encourages prayer, pilgrimage and conversation. This in turn contributes to what others find here.

We see something of this quest to relate to the divine in the buildings that were once here, and in those that remain. The island has been a place of Christian pilgrimage since the Irish saint Columba, Columcille – 'Colum of the church', founded a monastery here, in the mid-sixth century. In 1203 a Benedictine abbey was founded to replace the early Christian one, and at some stage before 1210 an Augustinian nunnery was also established. The life of these communities ended after the Reformation. The local people continued to work and pray on the island and to care for the ruins. The roofless abbey church was rebuilt a hundred years ago, and the abbey buildings during the mid-twentieth century.

Some of the prayers from earlier times that shaped the spiritual life of the island, or the culture from which that life came, are also included to offer an entry into how others have responded to the divine, in this place, in their time.

These poems, prayers and anecdotes are intended as an introduction, in translations that speak of the times in which they were written, to the richness of the spiritual traditions of those who worked, visited and worshipped here over many centuries. They are markers of the way of life and the aspirations of those who prayed them. From them we can learn how Columba's life and call were interpreted by his followers, and as they lived within the spiritual understanding of their own time.

Part One of this book reimagines the Columban monastery, which stood in various forms for 640 years. Columba died in 597 AD, and the changes every century after his death are considered in Chapters 1–8. The physical remains, artefacts and written

Nunnery chapel exterior.

sources increase the closer we get to its end, but much remains unknown.

The Columban period was followed by 350 years of Benedictine and Augustinian monastic life. The buildings changed over time, but they are more or less identifiable from their ruined or rebuilt state, and Chapters 9 and 10 focus on the physical remains.

Part Three, the Afterword, touches on what has happened to the ruined buildings since the Reformation, and to the other sites on the island that have been important in the past and present.

The first section includes poetry, prose and prayers associated with, and in some cases thought to have been made at, the early Christian monastery. Some of these works would have been known to the medieval monastic community. The second section includes similar material known to high medieval monastic communities, and which served as part of their regular spiritual diet.

On a dry day the Columban monastery is ideally explored from Tòrr an Abba, 'the abbot's hill', which gives a round view of the site. On a wet day it is suggested that the Columban section of the book can be considered from the rebuilt Saint Columba's shrine, which stands on the place that was for centuries the focus of the monastery.

The high crosses each merit a separate visit to explore their detail and the ways in which their original positions influenced how they were understood.

The Reilig Oran chapel connects the ancient and the medieval abbeys, and can be explored separately.

Part Two, Medieval Iona, considers in Chapter 9 first the rebuilt abbey church and cloisters, which are ideal for exploration on a wet day. The modern carvings on the cloister arcade can reward hours of attention for they are designed in a sequence that offers the viewer a reflective journey. Chapter 10 is an exploration of the nunnery, and is suited to lingering on a dry day.

The Afterword and the Further Reading are for those who wish to explore Iona's history, archaeology and literary output more deeply. The precise, specialist and laborious works undertaken by scholars and poets have been drawn upon in this brief guide, and their work provides the basis for deeper knowledge of the ways in which people have viewed Iona over the centuries.

In practical terms, Iona is a small Hebridean island, about 5 km long and 3 km wide, off the tip of the Isle of Mull. It has a resident population of about 100 people, and is reached by passenger foot ferry. The nunnery is about 200 metres and the abbey 700 metres from the landing place.

There are currently a number of residential centres, including one in the rebuilt abbey, where people can stay and engage with the ongoing spiritual life of the place. There are also a number of bed and breakfasts, two hotels, a hostel, and a small camping site.

The island is largely owned by the National Trust for Scotland, and most of it is farmed.

There are several sandy beaches and a number of minor sites, many of them within walking distance of the tarmac road. The staff of the Iona Community lead a pilgrimage around the island on most Tuesdays during the spring and summer months.

Iona.

PART ONE

Columban Iona

I

Iona before Columba

Iona is a small island in the Inner Hebrides, west of Mull, separated from it by a stretch of water some two kilometres wide. This has strong tides but the Sound of Iona had been preferred from ancient times to navigation through the much longer Sound of Mull.

The mountains of west Mull are nearly always partly visible from Iona, and on clear days the peak of the volcanically formed Ben More (966 metres) dominates the eastern skyline. To the north are small islands that include the Isle of Staffa, where Fingal's Cave was made famous by Mendelssohn in his Hebridean Overture. Beyond these islands, the Isle of Skye with its range of sharp volcanic peaks, the Cullins, can often be seen. To the west are the small Treshnish Islands, which, like Staffa, are now uninhabited but can be reached by boat from Iona. Most distinctive of them is Dutchman's Cap, a low-lying island with a central hump. Beyond is the Isle of Tiree and to its north, Coll. To the south, off Mull, lies the tidal island of Earraig, made known by Robert Louis Stevenson in his book *Kidnapped* as the place where David Balfour was shipwrecked. It has a line of nineteenth-century coastguard cottages, currently used by members of the Findhorn Community, who also have a white meditation booth on the cliffs of Mull facing Iona. Beyond can be seen Colonsay, Oransay and on a good day the hills of Jura.

As well as sandy beaches, the west of the island has a *machair*, a Gaelic term for a raised beach with light shell soils. This has been used for agriculture since the time of Saint Columba, most recently during the food shortages of the Second World War. Remnants of the lazy beds, parallel raised beds, fertilized with

This Latin poem, *Noli Pater*, is attributed to Columba, and the first six lines could date from his time.

Father, do not allow thunder and lightning,
lest we be shattered by its fear and its fire.

We fear you, the terrible one, believing there is none like you.
All songs praise you throughout the host of angels.

Let the summits of heaven, too, praise you with roaming
    lightning,
O most loving Jesus, O righteous King of Kings.

(Clancy and Márkus, 1995, p. 85)

seaweed and with drainage channels between them, can be seen, near what is now a golf course. There are small outcrops of marble on the south-east coast. There are also patches of raised bog, especially on the southern end of the island, where peat was harvested for fuel until recent times.

The natural world

There are no native land animals, though the seas provide seals and whales, sources of food in the past. There are otters, and also now mink, a North American species that has gone wild in the Hebrides.

Domestic animals have been brought in over the centuries and the island is grazed by cattle and sheep. Mice and rabbits (originally a food source) arrived with humans.

A number of migratory birds pass this way. Nesting birds include puffin, especially on the cliffs on the south-west shores. The island is home to the rare corncrake, whose croaking call may often be heard in spring and summer.

There are numerous wild plants, on the bog, the uplands, the shell sand of the west coast, and on the seashore.

Settlement

There is evidence from a shell midden of a very early, perhaps temporary, settlement on Iona. Also on the west of the island, north of the *machair*, is a promontory fort, a structure well known on the coasts of Ireland and western Scotland, the purpose of which is unknown.

A few artefacts have been found on the island but the constant habitation and reuse of sites since the sixth century has left evidence so complex that it is impossible to know how widely Iona was occupied in ancient times. The first population seems to have been visiting hunter-gatherers, seeking wild seeds and fruits, shellfish and inshore fish. Later, there was a settled farming community: there is evidence of Neolithic settlement on the east side of the island but we do not know how many people lived here, or for how long.

Parts of the *vallum*, the ditch-and-dyke formation of the monastery, in particular the parts beside the modern road north of the abbey, date from the first or second century AD. This suggests that the island had a significant role in earlier times, perhaps for religious reasons; and that an existing site was reused by Christian monks. About eight of the 2,000 or so acres of the island are enclosed within the monastic *vallum*.

Following the *vallum* south from the Macleod Centre, there is the faint outline of a ringed hut with a further ringed extension on its west end. Nearby, behind Dunsmeorach House (now owned by the Iona Community), there is a faint outline of a boat burial. The view is now obscured by the Columba Hotel but the burial points out over the Sound and south-east towards the rising sun.

The monastic vallum.

Both the surviving records of medieval Iona and reports of visitors in later centuries indicate that Iona was fertile by Hebridean standards. Cattle grazed and grain grew, in particular barley, the staple food.

Three slender strands that support the world:
the slender stream of milk into the pail,
the slender blade of corn in the ground,
the slender thread in the hand of a skilled woman.

Irish, eighth–ninth century (Meyer, 1911)

The name 'Iona'

Iona seems to have been uninhabited when Saint Columba arrived, traditionally in 563 AD, but the name might give some clues to its previous roles. The Gaelic name is Í, which appears to be from the Old Irish for 'eo', sacred tree, yew, making it the island of yew trees (Williams, 1989, pp. 423–4). The yew is one of the few native evergreens and a slow-growing tree whose wood was prized. Other such place names indicate clusters or even forests of yews. Places where yew grew, or was planted, often had religious significance before the arrival of Christianity.

The name could, however, come from another language now lost, from which it was borrowed by the Gaelic-speaking settlers from Ireland who had moved to south-west Scotland and its islands a few generations before Saint Columba arrived.

The seventh-century abbot Adomnán names the island in Latin, using a genitive form, as *ioua insula*, the island of Í. In his *Life of Saint Columba* Adomnán points out that in Latin 'columba' means 'dove', and so does the Hebrew *jona*. He continues:

For it is shown by the Gospels that the Holy Spirit descended upon the only begotten Son of the everlasting Father in the form of that little bird. For this reason, in the Scriptures the dove is generally taken allegorically to represent the Holy Spirit. Likewise, the Saviour himself in the Gospel told his disciples that they should have the simplicity of the dove in a pure heart. For the dove is indeed a simple and innocent bird, and it was fitting that a simple and innocent man should have this for his name, who throughout his dove-like life offered in himself a dwelling for the Holy Spirit.

(Adomnán, Sharpe, 2012, p. 104)

Columba in this way shares the name of the Old Testament prophet Jonah.

The name 'Iona' for the island is found in the late medieval period onwards. It appears to be derived from either a misunderstanding or a learned joke that connects the Hebrew word for dove, the name of the saint and the name of the island. Scribes often made the letters 'u' and 'n' similar, and someone copied the oblique case, *ioua*, as *iona*.

Irish or Scottish?

Modern political divisions, which place Iona in Scotland, did not pertain in the time of the Columban monastery. The south-west of Scotland had been settled from Ireland, and the Gaelic language of Ireland must have predominated. Further to the east was the Pictish kingdom, where another language was spoken; to the south a language related to Welsh was spoken; and south of this, in the Anglo-Saxon kingdoms the Germanic language we call Old English was used. In the liturgy and for scholarship and religious poetry, the international language, Latin, was used, both for writing, and to speak with learned visitors from other cultures. Early on, Gaelic, the native vernacular language, also began to be used in writing, for both religious and secular purposes.

The texts from the early Christian period have survived mainly in Ireland, or in those continental monasteries which received members from Ireland. Some are in Gaelic, and others in Latin. The Gaelic language for this period is usually called Old or Middle Irish, depending on linguistic forms which help to determine when the sources were first composed.

There was constant movement between the islands of the Hebrides and Ireland. During the times of Iona's Columban and medieval monastic foundations, and for many centuries afterwards, texts and oral stories passed across the sea. Some of the poems referred to in this book could have been composed in Iona or other parts of what is now Scotland.

2

To 597
Columba's Iona

The founder of the monastery on Iona was an Irishman of royal family, Columcille, 'Colum of the church'; in Latin, Columba. He is traditionally associated with Gartan in modern County Donegal, and was born about 523 AD. St Patrick had preached Christianity in Ireland only two generations previously. Columba is one of many early saints who are said to have spread the gospel and devoted themselves to setting aside places for the monastic life. In a society without towns, the first land north of the Roman Empire to receive Christianity, the monasteries provided focus and co-ordination for the Christian life.

We know about Columba from early Irish *Martyrologies*, lists of saints' feast days, which usually marked their day of death; and from three *Lives* written about him that show the traditions which grew up around him. One of these is the seventh-century biography by a successor as Abbot of Iona, Adomnán. This was written in Latin, and drew on sixth-century accounts, perhaps written, that had been collected from those who themselves remembered Columba. Another short *Life*, mainly a collection of miracles, was written in Irish during the tenth or eleventh century, a time when the lives of many Irish saints were composed. Finally, a compendium of traditions relating to him was produced in Irish in the early sixteenth century by Mánus Ó Domhnaill, a Donegal prince.

Adomnán himself was honoured as a saint, and had a *Life* composed about him in Latin centuries later. The names of other early abbots also appear in lists of saints.

Columba is said to have demonstrated a liking for the religious life from an early age. Adomnán takes Colum as his birth-name, though later sources say that he was at first named Crimthann, which means 'foxy'. This name was common at the time, but in scriptural terms might refer too closely to the King Herod whom Jesus termed 'that fox' (Luke 13.32). There is also a story about how his name Colum was lengthened to Colum Cille, Colum of the church, because he prayed frequently as a child.

Unlike his contemporaries he did not take to the normal life of young men of royal blood, a life of hunting and warfare, but became a monk and founded a number of monasteries, including one in Glencolmcille in south-west Donegal, and Durrow in the Irish midlands. Later, Derry, the port on Lough Foyle in north-west Ireland, was named as one of his foundations. As in other early Christian monasteries, the monks lived to a Rule, not unlike that of Saint Benedict, though harder.

Columba came to live and preach among the Irish settlers of south-west Scotland, according to the stories with a following, like Christ, of twelve men.

Why Columba came to Iona

No particular reason for this is given by his biographer Adomnán, writing a century after his time. The author says that in 563, at the age of 41 he left his homeland and spent his remaining 34 years as a pilgrim for Christ.

The medieval *Life* names many monastic houses he founded in Ireland, and then says that his desire for pilgrimage caused him to cross the sea to teach the word of God to 'Scots, Britons and Saxons'.

However, legends say that he left as an act of penitence. Adomnán himself says that for a time Columba was wrongly excommunicated in Ireland, though he does not specify the reasons. Columba left Ireland two years after the battle of Cúl Drebene, in modern County Sligo, fought by his royal kinsmen. It was said in the annals that his kinsmen prevailed through the saint's prayers. Some poems suggest that he was directly involved with the causes of the battle, and others refute such a suggestion. The most extensive account is recorded a thousand years after his time in the last of his *Lives* (see pages 101–2).

He may have left as an exile for Christ, relinquishing his status as far as possible, but also leaving aside the politics of his family's position. Among other visitors to Iona, an island relatively easily accessible by sea, there are stories of Columba's receiving penitents. Perhaps he was seen as an understanding ear, as one who had been through the experience himself. One of Iona's dependencies, the Isle of Canna, seems to have been a place where penitents could live out their exile and reparation with the support of each other.

Columba's choice of Iona, later attributed to his inability to see his beloved Ireland from the island, may have been because the site was already regarded as sacred.

View over the original abbey site.

There is a quatrain in the eleventh-century *Life of Saint Columba*:

Grey eye there is
That backwards looks and gazes
Never will it see again
Ireland's women, Ireland's men.

(Carney, 1985, p. 87)

Iona was the senior monastery in the loose association, or *familia*, of monasteries founded by Columba and dedicated to keeping his Rule. Columba himself visited Ireland again several times. From Ireland came the common language, the Latin books and the ideas. He also went on visits to the Picts and to their king whose fortress was near Inverness. The monastery at Portmahomack on the north-east coast may have been one of a number of daughter houses. In the following century, Iona also hosted a refugee member of the Northumbrian royal family, and in time seeded a monastery and preaching ministry to this large and powerful Saxon kingdom.

It is fairly certain that where the abbey is now was the central sacred space of the monastery. To recreate the early monastery as seen from Tòrr an Abba, the outcrop of rock where Columba is thought to have had a cell, the stone buildings must be replaced in the imagination with small structures of wood roofed with thatch.

These buildings have long since vanished. A small wooden church can be imagined, with room for some twelve or fourteen people to pray, probably facing each other, so they could chant the psalms in Latin antiphonally (one side and then the other taking a verse). There may have been other very small churches or chapels as well, the abbot's house, a scriptorium for writing, and a refectory nearby for communal meals.

Housing was basic – small cells shared by the monks, with room to sleep, write and little else. Columba himself seems to have had a cell for sleeping and another for study. Adomnán speaks of a place on a little hill from where he could see all that went on in the monastery. Archaeological work on Tòrr an Abba unearthed the base of a wooden structure built during the early period of the monastery. Various stones, placed there then or in later times, were taken to suggest a bed base and somewhere to write. Later, a cross was erected here, and numerous pebbles were found around it, perhaps offerings by later pilgrims who prayed here.

In the early Christian monastery, hours of study and prayer were long, and, as well as personal devotions, there was communal prayer, often including a night vigil. Columba is described as going away to the west of the island for personal prayer at the Hill of the Angels and no doubt other members of the community also went apart for times of intense prayer.

Columba was an avid copier of the Scriptures at a time when reading was rare, writing was rarer and there was a need to provide the texts with which to promote the spread of Christianity. He is described by Adomnán as writing up to the day of his death, copying the Psalter up to the line in what is now Psalm 34.10: 'Those that seek the Lord shall not want for anything that is good.'

One of the oldest of Irish manuscripts is the *Cathach*, a copy of the Bible's 150 psalms in Latin. It is ascribed to Saint Columba, and may indeed have been written by him, or in his honour after his death. Columba is also credited with being a poet, and some of his poems may be among the earliest writings of the monastery.

We can also imagine tilled land surrounding the central site, where wheat, barley and oats were grown, together with green vegetables, including brassicas and root vegetables. Food consisted mainly of fish, coarse porridge, seashore edibles and vegetables, and was prepared for visitors as well as the monastic community.

The markers of the monastic centre, the series of ditches and dykes, are similar to those surrounding a native secular building. Some parts of the *vallum* can be seen from Tòrr an Abba, and those on the left side of the road going north beyond the pottery show us something of their enormous scale.

This part of the *vallum* continues on the left of the road to the MacLeod Centre, and can be followed round until it branches, with one part ending in a cliff opposite the modern entrance. Excavations have shown that it continues along the line of the cemetery wall and down towards the sea. While the line of the *vallum*, and perhaps its internal size, changed over the centuries, this large enclosure would have kept animals out and provided room for vegetable gardens and space for craft workers and others who became associated with the monastery to work and live.

Although Columba and his relatives were aristocrats from a class-conscious society, Columba is described as engaging in manual labour, and expecting his monks to do the same. The Irish *Life* speaks of monks in Ireland doing the back-breaking task of hand grinding, something that was done in the wider society by slave women. We are told of an occasion when visitors were expected and Columba went to the mill to grind corn for them. This may have been a place where the work was done by hand, or it may have been a horizontal watermill of the kind introduced to Ireland from the Continent in the late sixth century. The small stream to the north of the abbey buildings, called the Mill-stream, was larger in the past, and remains of a mill of indeterminate age were found beside it, just above the craft-shop.

There was a boat to ferry visitors from the Isle of Mull – on still days people could call across the water to attract attention.

Fishing, and longer sea voyages, including the dangerous journey to Ireland, also took place.

Columba died on Iona in 597. His body was washed, wrapped and laid in the ground. The place would have been marked, with a stone or simple shrine. The site is probably where the current Saint Columba's chapel stands, at the west end of the medieval abbey. This became the focus of pilgrimage as well as veneration by the community.

As the 'place of his resurrection', the place from which his body would rise on the last day, many others desired to be buried on Iona, under his protection, just as a secular king would protect those who accepted his authority. His feast day, the day of his death, was 9 June.

The following is a translation of an alphabetical poem, *Adiutor Laborantium*, which is associated with Iona and attributed to Columba (though one of the editors has recently suggested it was by his biographer Adomnán (Márkus, 2010, pp. 145–61)). The lines each start with consecutive letters of the alphabet. The Latin original survived only in one copy in an Old English prayer book. An introduction says that Columba composed this poem on the way to the mill, while finding his sack of grain a heavy burden. The Latin has a regular rhythm suitable for plodding! It is also said that he composed his long poem *Altus Prosator*, the High Creator, while grinding corn in the mill to make bread for the monastery's visitors. This version has emulated the alphabetical structure of the original.

Adiutor Laborantium

Aid of the labourer,
Benefactor of good,
Custodian of defences,
Defender of believers,
Encouraging the humble and
Frustrating the proud:
Governor of the faithful,
Hostile to the impenitent,
Inquisitor of judges, and
Judge of wrong-doing:
Kindler of purest life,
Light, and father of light,
Magnificent in glory:
Never thwarting the hopeful, but
Offering strength and help,
Pity my weakness, my
Quivering wretchedness,

Rowing through the infinite
Storms of this age.
Take me and draw me, Lord,
Unto your kingdom blest,
Victor eternal.
With music most holy,
Exiting this world of sin,
You, leading me onward, to the
Zenith of heaven.

Through you, Christ Jesus, who live and reign ...

(Clancy and Márkus, 1995, pp. 72–3, adapted alphabetically by
Margaret Millar, used with permission)

3

To 697

An Age of Writing

At the beginning of this century, the oldest surviving poem in the Gaelic language, *Amra Coluim Cille*, a praise-poem (eulogy) in honour of the saint, is said to have been composed by a poet named Dallán Forgaill, whose name can be interpreted as 'dear blind witness'. It was one of the hymns recited on Iona.

From Tòrr an Abba we can imagine the monastery a century after Saint Columba's death. The buildings were still made of wood, but there were more of them, to cater for a larger community and for visitors.

Workers and craftspeople lived in the areas surrounding the sacred central space. There was tilled land for crops and gardens for vegetables, and space for poultry, cows and goats.

In the centre we can place the main church where members of the community met together for liturgy. There were other small churches as well, on the pattern of early monastic settlements founded from Ireland. Monks who were ordained said private liturgies while a community Mass was said on Sundays and for specific feasts.

The shrine of Saint Columba, patron, protector, model and intercessor with God, was central to monastic life. Perhaps it was already a simple stone shrine built over his grave, perhaps at this stage made of slabs raised at angles.

This shape was copied by metalworkers producing small portable shrines, to be carried on poles in procession, like the Monymusk reliquary, now in the National Museum of Scotland. This is a small shrine-shaped box, made in the eighth century,

Saint Cronán's church and shrine in County Clare.

and is believed to have contained relics of Saint Columba. Tradition links this to the Brecbennach, a small casket known in the Middle Ages, which was carried by the Scots forces at the Battle of Bannockburn in 1314.

The small stone, now known as Saint Columba's pillow, engraved with the ring-headed cross, was probably a grave-marker from this period.

Pilgrims came, but the monastery also provided sanctuary, under the protection of Saint Columba. One refugee was Oswald, of the royal family of Northumbria, the Saxon kingdom to the south-east of Iona. When he later was restored to kingship he asked for a monk of Iona to lead a mission to his own people. This led to the establishment in 635 AD of the monastery at Lindisfarne, Holy Island, and the start of the Christianization of this powerful kingdom.

Gospel books were brought to the kingdom, and new books were created in Northumbria. The most famous is the Lindisfarne

The Monymusk shrine.

Gospels, made at about the end of this century. In the following century the Englishman Bede was to record the story of the conversion of Northumbria, in Latin, which enabled it to be read throughout Europe. Adomnán visited Northumbria twice, and communications with Iona remained strong.

Writing and craft activities were a major part of the work on Iona. There was a scriptorium, where books were produced, and hymns and poetry composed on the island were written down.

Before the labour of copying each book by hand individually, there was the preparation of vellum on which to write. This required work by many members of the community. The monastery at Portmahomack in north-east Scotland, possibly one of the monasteries that Columba had founded in Pictland, was destroyed by fire in about 800 AD, and has recently been excavated. All the occupations involved in book-making took place on the same site. In spring there were new-born or young calves, which were slaughtered, their skins taken and put in a lime bath made from crushed and burnt seashells, then scraped, stretched, dried, smoothed and finally cut to size and lined for writing. Each calf yielded two pages, four sides, while smaller books were made of cut-down calfskin or from sheepskin or goatskin. The younger the animal the better was the quality of the finished product.

The poems of early Ireland speak of ink for writing made of oak or holly gall. Soot from fires was also used. Colours for embellishment were made from a number of locally produced and imported dyes.

On Iona in this century, there were two sites. The cobbled street of red Mull granite, called *Sràid nam Marbh*, the Street of the Dead, connects the burial ground to the monastery. It may be a replacement for an earlier street that connected the main site to a secondary one.

Just this side of the cemetery wall, an archaeological excavation uncovered the remains of a large circular wooden hut. Just behind it, the now-flattened monastic *vallum* showed evidence that holly had grown nearby, while the ditch held detritus, including fragments of leather for shoes and imported Mediterranean pottery. Found there was a small bronze bell, and evidence of glass and metalworking, matters associated with the covers or box-shrines for costly books, and container shrines for relics.

There were at least 25 books in the Iona library by the end of this century, apart from what was written here (Clancy and Márkus, 1995, pp. 211–22).

As well as copying the Scriptures and other works, the community occupied itself in writing records of major events. It is believed that such a record from Iona was later taken to Ireland where it formed the backbone of what is known as the *Annals of Ulster*.

There were also letters. One is known to have been written by a scholar called Cummian, and addressed to a hermit Beccán and the abbot Ségéne of Iona. It contained a report of how a synod in the south of Ireland in about 630 AD had agreed to the continental system of dating Easter, and responded to Ségéne's criticism of it.

At a time when the universal western Church worshipped together in Latin, it was considered desirable that it should as the Body of Christ celebrate the chief festivals together, especially the main one, the resurrection of Jesus. This occurred just after the spring equinox, and was calculated by adapting the Jewish lunar calendar date for the Passover. Ireland had followed an older calculation than was now used on the Continent, and Ségéne defended it. Not long afterwards, the controversy came to a head in Northumbria. At a synod in 664, vividly described three generations later by Bede, the continental dating for Easter was adopted. Iona, however, continued as it was.

One of Ségéne's successors was Adomnán, who in 679 became the ninth abbot. Like many of the early abbots, he was a member of the same royal family as Columba himself. His *Life of Saint Columba* was written about a century after the saint's own time. Unlike a modern biography, it assumes that the facts of the saint's life are well known. The *Life* describes him as a great writer, constantly surrounded by books, vellum and his inkhorn, writing until the end of his life, a model for the community in his industry. It also provides information about his miracles and sayings, for the edification of the listener. Some idea of the lifestyle and concerns of this saint and his followers can be deduced; how they farmed, what they ate, how they built, where they travelled, how they rested and what their prayer life was like.

Adomnán describes how Columba often went alone to pray. On one occasion, monks who followed him saw him conversing with angels. The hill facing the *machair* on the west coast, just south of the end of the road, is traditionally regarded as Adomnán's Hill of the Angels. High places in Europe are often associated with angels, especially the Archangel Michael, who defeated the devil.

In Adomnán's own time, in the course of a widespread severe drought, Columba's relics were carried round the island. Extracts from the books he wrote were read aloud at the Hill of the Angels 'where from time to time the citizens of heaven used to be seen coming down to converse with the saint' (Adomnán, 1991, p. 200). Heavy rain followed, the seed germinated and the prospect of a famine year was relieved.

Adomnán tells of Columba praying in the church at night, accompanied by a heavenly light that is too strong for others to bear. Like many saints, he banishes a water monster, perhaps a reference to the ways in which the people of the time were dependent on

The Hill of the Angels.

the seas and fresh waters for travel and for food, but aware of its dangers. In Columba's case, the action much impressed the Pictish people, for the monster was lodged in the short river that attaches Loch Ness to the sea. Columba is also depicted as having visions and foreknowledge, driving away plague-bearing demons, encouraging the labourers at harvest, welcoming guests and counselling penitents.

Adomnán travelled to the Irish monasteries founded by Columba, and also to Northumbria's Lindisfarne, where he stayed for some time. According to Bede, he was converted to the new dating of Easter, and attempted to introduce it to Iona, but failed. Durrow in central Ireland had accepted this date earlier in the century. Another trigger may have been that in 689 both calendars coincided. Adomnán retained a reputation as a peacemaker, in spite of the controversy.

There is a story of how Columba in his early years as a deacon tried and failed to save the life of a young woman who fled to him for protection (Adomnán, 1991, pp. 174–5). The fact that Adomnán includes this tale may point to his own concerns that respect is shown for places and for clerics, so that they in turn can provide protection, especially for the poor.

Adomnán promulgated the *Law of the Innocents* (Márkus, 2008), which was accepted by leading figures at a synod at Birr in central Ireland in 697 AD, a hundred years after Columba's death. This work, written in Irish for a secular as well as a clerical audience, brought women, children and clerics under the protection of rulers as non-combatants in the endemic warfare of the time. According to later accounts, it also released women from any requirement to take part in military activity. It was numbered among the three Laws of Ireland: Saint Patrick's law, not to kill clerics; Adomnán's law, not to kill women; and the nun Dáire's law, not to kill cattle (Stokes, 1905, p. 211). The cattle were the source of food, especially for the young or weak.

This quatrain in Old Irish is attributed to Adomnán, and is recorded in his tenth-century *Life*:

If I be destined to die in Iona,
it were a merciful leavetaking.
I know not under the blue sky
A better little spot for death.

(Clancy and Márkus, 1995, p. 167.
From *Betha Adamnán*, Herbert and Ó Riain, 1988, p. 61)

Adomnán also wrote a book on the holy places. This is based on the memoirs of a Frankish (West European) bishop called Arculf, who came to Iona after having made a pilgrimage to Jerusalem and the other places associated with Christ's life on earth.

Churches on Iona as elsewhere identified with the place of the first resurrection, of Jesus, at the Holy Sepulchre. The great round church had been built by the emperor Constantine at the place where his mother Saint Helena had found the 'true cross'. The sketches Arculf made may have been used as the basis for some of the illustration pages in the *Book of Kells*.

Much of this writing, as well as the work of the craftspeople, may have gone on in the area where the large hut stood, to the abbey side of the wall. Perhaps the cemetery itself was already in use, consecrated as a holy place. Later stories connect it with a Saint Oran, companion of Columba. Later, it was known as a burial ground for kings, and perhaps, like other small burial sites on the island, for pilgrims and for those who were not monks but worked for the monastic community.

Adomnán died in 704 and was himself venerated, appearing in early Irish lists of saints. In about the tenth century, a *Life of Adamnán* was composed, probably at Kells in the Irish Midlands. Adomnán is depicted among other things as freeing hostages, protecting clerics, and judging mercifully a woman who kills another woman. He is also seen nursing the baby Jesus in his cell.

The following extract comes from the *Alphabet of Devotion*, Aipgitir Chrábaid, a work in Old Irish on the religious life. It is attributed to the nephew of Columcille, Colmán, Abbot of Lynally in County Offaly.

Faith together with works,
eagerness together with steadfastness,
tranquillity together with zeal,
chastity together with humility,
fasting together with moderation,
poverty together with generosity,
silence together with conversation,
division together with equality,
patience without resentment,
detachment together with nearness,

fervour without harshness,
mildness together with fairness,
confidence without carelessness,
fear without despair,
poverty without arrogance,
confession without excuses,
teaching together with fulfilling,
climbing without falling,
being low towards the lofty,
being smooth towards the harsh,
work without grumbling,
guilelessness together with prudence,
humility without laxity,
religion without hypocrisy –
    all these things are contained in holiness.

It is when full of charity that one is holy.
He walks in charity.
Every evil fears him;
every good loves him.
He has honour upon earth;
he has glory in heaven ...

(Carey, 2000, p. 233)

4

To 797
A Century of Art

Two centuries after Columba's death, the monastery was thriving. The shrine can now be imagined as elaborate, and contained within a tiny free-standing church, the size of the current Columba's chapel, or even smaller. During this century, the older monastic buildings surrounding it were slowly replaced with stone ones, longer-lasting structures less subject to the danger of fire. We can imagine where the abbey church now stands a number of small cells and a larger church, with other smaller churches nearby. All, like the shrine chapel of Saint Columba, were separate free-standing buildings, first of wood, then of mortared stone.

There was also ongoing activity the abbey side of the Reilig Oran, and the burial ground was one of several satellite burial grounds, each probably with their own small chapel.

It seems likely that the liturgy of the Eucharist was commonly celebrated within small churches, during the early Christian period. Perhaps only one or two attendants were with the priest, and the sacred elements were then brought to the larger community waiting outside.

There may have been a small stone chapel on the island, about 300 metres to the south, where the present Saint Ronan's chapel stands beside the nunnery. Excavations under parts of the floor in 1992 indicated a small structure under the present building, which had been covered in a white lime mortar. Underneath that, there were burials. This suggests that this was a holy place, a burial ground, from early in the monastery's life (O'Sullivan,

1994). Standing apart from the main monastery, it is possible that it was for secular burials, perhaps for people who worked for the Columban monastery, perhaps for women, and perhaps for pilgrims. Another burial ground is believed to have been near where the current Church of Scotland parish church stands, beyond Saint Columba's Hotel, while there was an early burial ground further south by Martyrs' Bay.

The monastery on Iona might have been too busy for some members. Perhaps as part of a reform movement that swept across the Irish monastic world, another centre was founded at Clàdh an Disert, the 'hermitage burial ground', a little to the north of the main site but within the enclosure. The outline of a later stone church can be seen here. Also, marking an entrance, were two standing stones which supported a lintel until about 200 years ago.

The word *disert* is a loan word, 'desert', and the lifestyle was based on that of the Desert Fathers, the early Christian hermit monks of North Africa. Austere ascetic practices and a rigorous life of prayer were adopted. These ascetic monks had ordained members, as did the main community. We do not know whether some monks went apart to follow the ascetic life for a time, or lived as hermits, and then returned to the main community.

Meanwhile, links with other monasteries in the 'family' of Saint Columba continued. The English mission had flourished, and during this century some of the story of Iona was told by the great English writer Bede.

His aim was to show Christianity as a uniting force, among the peoples of the English-speaking kingdoms, and ideally among all the peoples of both islands, for all were part of the universal church. For this reason, issues that differed, such as the use of the ancient system of dating Easter, brought by Columba, were significant. The great set-piece of Bede's *Ecclesiastical History of the English People* is the recreation of the debate at Whitby in the Northumbrian kingdom in the year 664. At this, the modernized dating of Easter used by the continental churches, was accepted, together with other changes. To Bede this was the right outcome: the universal church which looked each year to Christ's bringing back the light, at his resurrection, could be celebrated across the world on the same date. Other English kingdoms adopted this dating a few years later at the Synod of Hertford in 673.

Bede notes that Adomnán had tried unsuccessfully to promote the new calculation on Iona and in the Columba monasteries of Ireland, before his death in 704 AD.

During the seventh century much of the south of Ireland had accepted the continental dating, and in 716 so did Iona. In 719 Iona also adopted the continental monastic haircut of a shaving of the scalp rather than the front of the head.

Northumbria had benefited from its long contact with Iona, and this continued. One of the results was the development of written works in the local vernacular, English, as well as Latin.

Changes continued on Iona. Flat stones, often sea-washed, were used to mark graves, and some bear incised crosses. The stylized cross with a ringed head had emerged, and several slabs in the museum show signs of being adorned with interlaced patterns as well.

The ring-head design may have developed from the stylized Chi-Rho, the first two letters for Christ in Greek, XP, or the first three, XPI, where the final letter is absorbed into the stem of the P. The ring-head is formed when the X is made an upright cross, and the ring of the P is centred around the cross.

The other possibility is that the ring-headed cross is a local version of a design used on the Continent in late-classical times. This is the *Christus victor*, Christ triumphant, the cross carrying the Roman laurel of victory.

At some time in this century, free-standing high crosses began to be raised. The great high crosses are later named in association with particular saints, and it may be that this was the case from early times.

From Tòrr an Abba we can see where the high crosses were intended to stand in the landscape. Much of their detail is intricate, and needs to be considered from close-up as well.

Saint John's cross

Saint John's cross stood a few paces west of Saint Columba's shrine, and was perhaps raised before a stone building was there. In the cross base today there stands a concrete replica of the original. This last blew down in the 1950s, and the fragments have been re-erected in the museum.

Making a cross with a wingspan of nearly 2 metres was ambitious. Saint John's cross is also slender. It stood as a powerful and elegant statement of faith, visible across the Sound of Iona, marking the sacred centre of the monastery, the tomb of Saint Columba.

Originally, the cross had circular 'armpits' where the cross-pieces join, but no ring. It fell early in its history, and it is thought that rings were added to strengthen it. The cross was blown down several times, even after the medieval abbey gave it some shelter.

The fine grain of stone allowed the carving of small-scale scenes. Most noticeably, Saint John's cross is crawling with intertwined snakes, rising upwards. Many form a saltire cross, an 'X' as they move up the shaft.

Although Iona, like Ireland, has no native snakes, Adomnán says Columba blessed Iona so that the poison of snakes will have no power to harm people or their livestock as long as those who live here keep Christ's commandments (Adomnán, pp. 177, 225).

Behind this is the story of the people of Israel in the desert, complaining of the snakes that bit them (Numbers 21. 6–9). Moses was commanded to make a bronze snake, and those who gazed upon it would be healed. Jesus, the new Moses, says that he will be raised up like the serpent in the desert and will draw all people to himself (John 3.13–14 and 12.32). The snake, which sloughs off its skin and renews itself, represents the redeemed Christian being raised up towards Christ.

Saint John's cross replica.

Saint Oran's cross

This massive cross has no ring, though it has 'armpits' that give the sense of a ring. Broader than the Saint John's cross but with as wide a wingspan, it is thought to have stood at the entrance to the central holy site, a few paces north of the Reilig Oran chapel. The cemetery wall now closes what was an entrance through the ditch and dyke of the *vallum*. The cobbled street led through this entrance between the main site and the secular burial ground.

There is a large stone cross base against the outside wall of the chapel, of the size that held the Saint Oran cross in earlier times.

The cross is said to have been rediscovered in fragments in the ruined Saint Oran's chapel, during the nineteenth century. It is not known when it fell, but one side is much damaged by water, which suggests it was lying in the open for some time during the last 1,200 years.

On the best-preserved face, just below where shaft and arms meet, there is the image of the Virgin Mary, seated, with the child Jesus in her arms. There is intimacy in the pose, as he turns towards her. The childlikeness and humanity of Jesus is depicted in the delicately dangling feet. Two angels hover by the Virgin's head.

Perhaps this side of the cross may have been deliberately placed face-downwards to hide the Virgin and child, in the hope that it would survive during Reformation times.

One of the broken fragments of a smaller cross in the museum also has the dangling feet, and perhaps held a similar scene.

The Saint Oran cross is in the museum, where it was raised again in 2013.

Virgin and child, Saint Oran's cross.

37

The poetry of early Ireland has given delight again during the last century of translations.

Learned in music sings the lark,
I leave my cell to listen;
His open beak spills music, hark!
Where heaven's bright cloudlets glisten.

And so I'll sing my morning psalm
That God bright heaven may give me
And keep me in eternal calm
And from all sin relieve me.

Eighth–tenth century (Flower, 1947, p. 54)

The pose on the Saint Oran cross is very similar to that in the Virgin and child illumination in the *Book of Kells*. It was perhaps in honour of the bicentenary of Columba's death that Iona's most ambitious project began at the end of the century.

This great Gospel book, which is lavishly illuminated, must have been a major venture for a community, even one accustomed to creating books. The richness and variety of the colours, and the artistic skills are obvious, even at a casual glance, but there is no precedent for the deep theology that lies behind the illuminations.

The Book contains the Four Gospels and some related matter. The preliminary pages are fully illuminated, and the plan was to have at least three full-page illuminations to introduce each Gospel, together with full-page illuminations for major liturgical events. Profoundly moving, it is the work of people aware of complex theology who also had the imagination and artistic ability to express it visually. The ways in which the Scriptures were made attractive, in places fun, is something that has only recently begun to be to be understood again.

Many people worked upon it, scribes, artists and unidentifiable assistants. A single great mind must lie behind a project that called upon the labour and skills of the whole community, and relied on the influences from abroad as well as from within the tradition. The people who did the work are anonymous, though we know the name of one possible candidate, a scribe and bishop of Iona called Connachtach who died in 802. It was never finished.

This great work started at the very end of this century. So did another matter, one that prevented the *Book of Kells* from ever being completed, and which was to bring generations of disruption, destruction and fear.

5

To 897

A Century of Disruption

At the start of this century, much of the monastery we have imaginatively reconstructed was suddenly laid waste.

In 793, without warning, Vikings attacked Lindisfarne, the monastery founded from Iona in the kingdom of Northumbria. Other monasteries were also pillaged. Iona itself was attacked in 795. The community must have been living in fear.

Perhaps the monastic *vallum*, the marker of the sacred site under the protection of Columba, was fortified at this time, raised, repaired and stockaded against those to whom the saint's protection meant nothing. In 802 there was another raid and the monastery was burnt down. Four years later, there was another attack and 68 members of the community were slain.

The dead may have been protecting the monastery against Vikings running amok. They may have been trying to hide the relics, books and other treasures, including the shrines which the Vikings prized for their precious metals and stones, and the fine artistic work.

The monastery's inhabitants would have feared being taken as slaves, for the Vikings traded their captives across Europe. In 1957 an excavation in what is now the abbey cloisters, and was then part of the central sacred space of the Columban monastery, came upon a mass grave of very young men, buried together hastily. Some were too young to have wisdom teeth, and they showed signs of having died violently (Thomas, 1957, p. 13, Cowie, 1995). One lad still had his finger in his mouth, and his jaw smashed through his skull.

Perhaps some of these young men had been working on the *Book of Kells* and similar great books. This work, treated as a relic in its own right, was one of the items that escaped the onslaught. This suggests that plans had been made to hide the chief treasures and protect them from fire.

In 806 land was obtained in east-central Ireland at Kells, and building started there the following year. By 814 a stone church had been raised, and key members of the community departed from Iona to what then became the main house of the Columban federation of monasteries. The great unfinished Gospel book is likely to have been one of the treasures taken with them. The fact that certain pages were left unfinished may be in honour of those who had their crucifixion on Iona.

A community remained on the island. In 825, in another raid, a monk named Blathmac was killed violently when he refused to say where the costly shrine covering the relics of Saint Columba was hidden. This event is the subject of a eulogy far away in central Europe, in the abbey of Reichenau in Lake Constance, by the abbot, the poet Walafrid Strabo. The story suggests that by this time the raiders knew what they particularly wanted and had an interpreter.

There were other raids. It may be because of them that in 847 some relics were taken to safety, to Dunkeld in inland Scotland, where a community had been founded in honour of Saint Columba.

This was a time of turbulence across northern Europe. The Vikings came from Scandinavia, and may have been driven by hunger for land as well as wealth. They were skilled seafarers with ships that could be beached, then floated off as the tide turned. The Vikings traded across Europe and beyond. At a time when many societies had slaves, they found ready markets for human beings as well as for the goods and foodstuffs they looted. The places they headed for, especially on the coasts, had few defences against those who did not know of the saints' protection, nor cared for their wrath. Further, many Viking attacks appear to have been frenzied. A ninth-century Irish quatrain says:

Bitter and cold the wind tonight
It tosses the sea's white hair;
Tonight I fear not the fierce Vikings
Coursing the Irish Sea.

Yet they did not come every year, and the community must have been on the lookout for them, ready to flee, resist, or at least hide themselves and their portable treasures. Even so, staying on a small island must have taken a high level of tenacity, a belief in the value of continuing monastic life. It could end violently one night, through death or enslavement and transportation to unknown lands and demands.

Yet the monastery continued to attract pilgrims and some people stayed. Kenneth MacAlpin, the king associated with the Dunkeld foundation, may also have initiated the practice of burying Scottish kings on Iona. In a century where people lived with the threat of violence, the usual events, like funerals, also occurred, the harvest was gathered and pilgrimage continued.

The reliquary of Saint Columba's remains seems to have been portable, as it was hidden at times of danger. Saint Columba's shrine chapel we can imagine as restored and rebuilt to house it, and other stone buildings raised in place of the burnt wooden ones. We do not know if there was ever a round tower as there was at Kells, a bell tower to sound the hours of prayer, to hold valuables and foodstuffs, and perhaps also to display relics from a high doorway to crowds of pilgrims.

Contact with Ireland seems to have been much lessened, first by the raids themselves and the depletion of the community and its resources that must have followed; but also by the move of the abbots to Kells. However, relics and people continued to move to and fro.

Agricultural life continued, for monks and pilgrims needed to be fed. Contact seems to have continued in other fields, even if sporadically. In time, as the Norse settled in the Hebrides, Iona came more and more within their ambit, and slowly acquired their protection.

During this century, the carving of the high crosses continued. Some of the Iona high cross carvings show similarities to crosses in Ireland, and also in Islay, the southern Hebridean island that looks across to the northern coast of Ireland. Islay had long been associated with the Iona monastery, and was probably already what it was to become, a seat of secular power for the Norse Kingdom of Man and the Isles.

Saint Martin's cross

Saint Martin's cross still stands on its original base where it was first raised. It is carved out of a single piece of granite (epidoritite). On the east side there is a complex interlace arrangement of snakes and bosses, while the west side contains biblical scenes, and on the cross head are the figures of the Virgin and child, with four angels.

The cross is not of such fine stone as Saint John's cross, but the carving shows a high degree of skill and a depth of theological understanding.

The outline is different to the earlier crosses, with a much narrower cross head. Looking at the sides, we can see a break in the abstract decoration. Above this is a perfectly proportioned Greek cross, and below it an extended stem.

The top of the cross and the ends of the arms contain slots in which wooden extensions may have been placed. These would serve to restore the normal outline of a high cross, while weighing much less than stone, making the cross more stable. But these slots may have instead held gold and other adornments, perhaps ones that could be removed and hidden if needed. The cross itself, raised between Viking attacks, shows no sign of damage other than that inflicted by the weather of twelve centuries.

The scenes on the west face have a sequence to them. At the base there is a panel with snakes, representative perhaps of the redeemed Christians being drawn up to Christ, surrounding oval bosses set in threes, a reminder of the Trinity. Above are four human figures. The one on the left, perhaps a woman, relates to the figure on her right, who blesses her, or the onlooker. The next figure stands and receives a greeting from a kneeling or sitting figure. These might suggest Mary meeting Elizabeth and Hannah being blessed by the high priest. The Old Testament story foreshadows the New Testament one, for Hannah is pregnant with the future high priest Samuel, and Mary with Jesus, the ultimate high priest.

Above them, David, the shepherd-king from Bethlehem, plays a large harp, and is accompanied by a smaller angel. The image perhaps refers both to Christ as king, and to the daily work of the monastery, the recitation of the psalms, which David was thought to have composed.

Above them, a panel depicts the cost of faith. Abraham holds a sword and seems to bless Isaac, who places wood on an altar. The angel is present to prevent the father sacrificing the son, but there is no sign of the ram that replaced Isaac.

Above them is a figure embraced by two animals. This may be Daniel in the lions' den, and perhaps also Christ after his baptism, in the wilderness with the wild beasts.

The Virgin and child above them are in a different pose to that of the Oran cross. Here, Mary is presenting the child outwards to the onlookers as she once presented him to the wise men who came with gifts. As in the *Book of Kells*, four angels surround them. Also on this level, the arms carry carvings of lions, often used as a reference to Christ, while on the shaft above the arms, serpents rise upwards towards the sky.

The west face of the cross therefore tells the story of the incarnation of Jesus and the presentation of him by Mary, first to the Gentile Magi, as seen on similar crosses in Islay and at Kells, and then to us, the onlookers. This image has stood through attacks by Vikings, and remained in its original site when the Benedictine abbey was built nearby.

The sun caught different scenes at different hours of the day, and the scenes may have been chosen specifically to relate to the worship of that particular hour in the monastic routine. The setting sun catches the Virgin and child while the lower scenes are already in shadow.

After the Reformation, two travellers, Martin Martin in the 1690s and the Irish bishop Thomas Pocock in 1760, recount that the people of the island buried their stillborn children around the foot of this cross. Unlike the islanders, they do not seem to have noted that the central figure was Mary with her child.

Saint Martin's cross.

Cantemus in omni die, 'Let us sing every day': A monk of Iona
composed this hymn, in Latin, it is thought in about the year 700.

Mary of the Tribe of Judah,
Mother of the Most High Lord,
gave fitting care
to languishing mankind.

Gabriel first brought the Word
from the Father's bosom
which was conceived and received
In the Mother's womb ...

Let us put on the armour of light,
the breastplate and helmet,
that we may be perfected by God,
taken up by Mary.

Truly, truly, we implore,
by the merits of the Child-bearer,
that the flame of the dread fire
be not able to ensnare us.

Let us call on the name of Christ,
below the angel witnesses,
that we may delight and be inscribed
in letters in the heavens.

From *Cantemus in omni die* (Clancy and Márkus, 1995, pp. 182–5)

6

To 997
A Time of Decline?

During this century, on the parts of the island that we see from Tòrr an Abba, the *vallum* may have been fortified, though it is a large area to defend. We do not know how far the *vallum* stretched on the seaward side, or whether there were other defences. The Vikings traditionally beached on sandy shores, and are associated in local tradition with the North Strand.

The community had its churches, domestic buildings and stores; a guest house, accommodation for penitents, royal and otherwise, perhaps craftspeople, and an active if diminished community. There may still have been the ascetic Celí Dé and hermits on the island.

For all the terror, the rebuilding and agricultural life went on; so did the visits, the pilgrimages, the funerals. The stone crosses remained standing. Poetry also continued. A quatrain in Irish from about this time says:

> There is here above the brotherhood
> a bright tall glossy yew;
> the melodious bell sends out a clear keen note
> in St Columba's church.

(Jackson, 1935, p. 10)

Life was changing for the Norsemen too. In 870 the Norwegian king Harald Finehair is said to have claimed the Hebrides as his own, and by the tenth century there were certainly considerable settlements of Scandinavians in the Islands. Their lifestyle must have included commerce and common interests as well as violence. They first came with a different language, religion and culture, but from this century there are graveslabs indicating that people of Norse name were buried on Iona according to Christian rites. Some slabs have their names in the runic alphabet of the Scandinavian peoples.

There are written records of others, like Óláfr *kvaran*, Norse king of Dublin, who ended his life here in the year 980. Not long afterwards, according to the Icelandic saga of Norway's King Óláfr Tryggvasson, the court poet Hallfreðr *vandrœðaskáld*, Hallfred the Troublesome Poet, an Icelander who reluctantly converted to Oláfr's Christian religion, died at sea. At peace at last with his new faith, his wave-driven coffin came to the shores of Iona for burial.

This was *ey in helga*, the holy island, to the Norsemen. By the end of the century, due to active conversion or the forceful persuasion of their rulers, the Norsemen were adopting Christianity. But it may be significant that none of the members of the monastic community are known to have had a Norse name.

Not all the descendants of the Vikings lived to Christian requirements regarding the sacred. In 980, the *Annals of Inisfallen* report:

Í Coluim Chille was plundered by foreigners, and the Isles were devastated by them, and they slew the bishop of Í.

Then, on Christmas Eve in 986, the abbot and sixteen of the community were slain.

The royal secular burial ground of Reilig Oran may have been busy these years. By a tradition mentioned first in the twelfth century, kings of Scotland were buried here from time immemorial, brought from the small island of Inch Kenneth off the west coast of Mull, and to shore at Martyrs' Bay.

Martyr here means 'witness' one who had died at peace in Christ. Inch Kenneth is named after Saint Canice, *Cainnech*, one of the Twelve Apostles of Ireland, who is said to have founded a small monastic settlement here. He was reputed to be a friend of

Martyrs' Bay.

Saint Columba, and one of the satellite burial grounds on Iona is named Kil-Chainnech.

Irish kings were also buried here, for the Annals refer to royal pilgrimages that ended on Iona, with a life of penance. The four kings of Norway said to be buried on the island, are however unknown.

The monastery at this period probably contained more small stone buildings. The small Columba's shrine may have been rebuilt, and perhaps, except when hidden for safety, the relics that remained on the island were preserved here, perhaps in an upper loft accessible by ladder. Columba's *flabellum*, his staff of office (in origin a Middle-Eastern fly-swatter), was kept on the island when not on loan to other monasteries, until lost overboard in the eleventh century.

There were buildings for the monastic community, perhaps stone cells like those of Ireland. Book copying would no doubt have continued whenever the raw materials were available. Clothes needed to be made, and the descendants of the Vikings may well have increased the variety of goods available by trade that could be used for writing and decorating. Their sea knowledge may have improved other areas of life, such as travel, and the provision of food, by fishing further out to sea.

Contact was kept between Iona's monastery and the house at Kells, and with the dependencies and rental lands in the Hebrides and on the western seaboard of the mainland, that paid rent in goods and agricultural produce.

The main sources for our knowledge about food are early Irish laws from the seventh and eighth centuries which give an idea of what was available, except during famine, and what kind of food was deemed suitable to people of each social class. The laws give an idea of what kind of crops were grown, who ran a mill to grind the corn, rights of access through other people's lands, and how other forms of work, which must have been communal, like road-making, were undertaken.

In this society, laws were a socially binding force, providing cohesion and outlining what was acceptable. Most social transgressions could be amended by the payment of set fines, depending on social status, and with the system weighted in favour of those of high status.

The Penitentials, lists suggesting suitable penances for moral transgressions, are based on these law codes, and are intended as guidelines to give a sense of the seriousness of different kinds of sin. Instead of fines, penitential practice was regarded as a form of spiritual medicine suitable to the transgression. For penitents, there was the possibility of living a restricted life for a certain length of time before returning to a society which had had time to cool down. The penitent also often had the advantage of going through the restrictions in community with others.

In some cases, in the Penitentials the civil law is upended, and penances for certain sins are much more severe for those of higher status in the religious life. The Christian message of the equality of all people before God, and the need for charity, overrides the laws and points out that those with power and status are called more severely to account.

There was also the example of people like Saint Columba, who had chosen exile, the worst penalty that could be dealt out to a free man, for the love of God.

Saint Matthew's cross

Though only pieces have survived, this is the last of the great high crosses from the early Christian monastery. It stood close to Saint Martin's cross, at the west end of the abbey. The huge, stepped, cross base is still there, but the remainder of the cross, the lower part of the shaft and a few fragments, was taken under cover during recent years, and is in the museum.

Raised on this site before the abbey was built to its immediate east, the imagery of this cross can be read in conjunction with that of the older Saint Martin's cross, as part of the drama of creation, seen again each morning.

Saint Matthew's cross, east face with Eden scene.

As the Columban monks left their night offices by the door at the west end of their church, they would have seen by the early morning light the lowest scene on the east face of the Saint Matthew cross.

Here there is a large image of Adam and Eve and between them the tree of life. At the beginning of the day is a reminder of the start of humanity. Our first parents look outwards towards us, with the tree of eternal life between them.

The serpent is also present, head down and slinking away defeated, only to be trapped in an interlace pattern. As in the *Book of Kells*, the interlace with no beginning and no end acts as a barrier to evil. Here, evil is present but defeated, trapped in the world but without a place in the life in Christ brought about by the cross and resurrection of Jesus. The story which started in a garden will end in the holy city, of which the monastery is a human preliminary.

The rays of the morning sun would also have touched the entwined snakes and bosses of the east face of Saint Martin's cross, the cross of Christ drawing all humanity to himself.

There were other crosses, and a number of stone cross bases lie around the abbey and nunnery. One stood on Tòrr an Abba, where the cross base can still be seen. Another is said to have stood overlooking the landing-place at Martyrs' Bay into the nineteenth century. Others may have been made of wood and have perished, like the cross Adomnán says Saint Columba made as a stopping place between the monastery and the fields on the west coast *machair*. Crosses marked the boundaries of the sacred precincts or would have provided resting places for people to pray on their way to and from the shrine to Saint Columba. Perhaps some of them were also the focus of outdoor communal liturgies.

In the middle of this century, a life of Adomnán was written, probably at Kells. It was written in Adomnán's honour, but it is also a warning for its own time on the good conduct required of kings, towards the monastic life and towards upholding the laws. Kells was pillaged around this time by the Norse of Dublin, perhaps with the support of the high king, in whose personal territory Kells was. Adomnán was recalled with great respect, and his roles in politics and social justice are emphasized. Just as he was effective in his time, persuading the powerful to protect the weak, he continues to protect his own, and the weak, by interceding for them in heaven. A member, like Columba, of a royal house, and like Columba one who gave up secular power to follow the life of prayer, he is a warning on the right use of power for those in the author's own time.

Stories regarding Columba himself were still being created, and while Iona was remote compared to Kells and Derry, it remained significant. In the mixed Norse-Gaelic world of the Hebrides, Iona was important, a stopping point for travellers, and a refuge in times of war and famine, at least where Christian practice led to respect of the sacred nature of the site.

Saint Columba remained the muse in the poetry from this century.

This were pleasant, O Son of God,
with wondrous coursing
to sail across the swelling torrent
back to Ireland.

To Eólarg's plain, past Benevanagh,
across loch Feval,
and there to hear the swans in chorus
chanting music.

And when my boat, the Derg Drúchtach,
at last made harbour
in Port na Ferg the joyful Foyle-folk
would sound a welcome.

I ever long for the land of Ireland
where I had power,
an exile now in midst of strangers,
sad and tearful.

Woe the journey forced upon me,
O King of Secrets;
would to God I'd never gone there,
to Cooldrevne.

Well it is for the son of Dimma
in his cloister,
and happy I but were I hearing
with him in Durrow

the wind that ever plays us music
in the elm-trees,
and sudden cry of startled blackbird,
wing a-beating.

And listen early in Ros Grencha
to stags a-belling,
and when cuckoo, at brink of summer,
joins in chorus.

I have loved the land of Ireland
– I cry for parting;
to sleep at Comgall's, visit Canice,
this were pleasant.

Eleventh-century Irish (Carney, 1985, pp. 82–7)

Loch Feval is Lough Foyle, on which Derry, the oak grove, the site
of a major Columban monastery and the principal port, was situ-
ated. Cooldrevne is the scene of the battle to which is attributed
Columba's departure for Iona. Durrow is a Columban monastery
in central Ireland. Elm was one of the 'noble trees' of Ireland,
useful for many things. The names of early saints, said to be
contemporary with Columba are given.

7

To 1098
Renewal and Refocus?

We can imagine in this century the stone buildings in place but the population associated with the island and monastery perhaps low in number, and the buildings in need of attention. Columba's chapel was standing, and a place for the abbot, a guest house and other buildings, such as a refectory, may be imagined.

The cemetery at Reilig Oran may have had elaborate stone slabs on some of the graves. Members of the monastic community may have had their graves, some also marked, around the main site.

Little is known of the start of the century, but its end saw several notable events. It may have seemed that the way of life was returning to what it had been before the disturbance caused by the Vikings.

Columba's reputation remained as strong as ever, in Ireland and in Scotland as well as locally. This century saw the writing of the *Life* in Irish, which brings together traditions about the saint. The length suggests that it could be read aloud in its entirety, as a homily in church or over a meal.

The tradition of burying Scottish nobles and kings continued. Macbeth, known to many from Shakespeare's play, and his predecessor King Duncan, are both said to be buried on Iona.

In 1069 Macbeth's successor Malcolm Canmore ('large head') married Princess Margaret, who had fled to Scotland following the conquest of her native England by William of Normandy. A radical church reformer, Margaret established Dunfermline as the centre of royal church activity.

Though respectful of the piety of the old monastic way of life, Margaret ensured that many Scottish foundations transferred to following continental Rules, such as that of the Augustinian canons. According to the *Life* written by her friend Turgot, later Bishop of Saint Andrews, she also argued against other practices, including a 'barbarous rite' practiced in some parts of Scotland. This may have included saying parts of the liturgy in the local language instead of Latin. Margaret appears to have been devout, ordered, strict on herself and her family, but well-loved. A well-educated woman, but with no knowledge of the Gaelic language and apparently little interest in its traditions, she used her knowledge of Scripture and Church tradition to make her points, and her husband often acted as translator.

She made no changes to the way of life on Iona but repaired the buildings, which had fallen into decay.

Margaret and Malcolm died within days of each other in 1093, and were both buried at Dunfermline. During the years following, Domnall *bán*, Malcolm's brother, made two bids for the kingship and was himself eventually buried in the traditional manner on Iona, the last Scottish king to rest here.

Margaret's biographer Turgot had once been tutor to King Óláfr the Peaceful of Norway. In 1098 his son King Magnús Barelegs, great-nephew of King Óláfr the Saint, swept down upon the Hebrides, looting and burning. Having pillaged his way south, Magnús arrived on Iona, where he went ashore and looked into the 'little church of Columcille'. Immediately he closed the door, forbade anyone else to enter and told his men not to harm the island. He then went on to Mull, which he pillaged, and continued southwards in this vein. Magnús was killed in Ireland in 1103. The accounts of his visit to 'the holy island', Iona, were written some 120 years later, but they contain poetry which mentions Iona, and this was probably composed at the time of these events.

Saint Columba's chapel

This little chapel, some three metres in length and half that in breadth, is at the centre of Iona's sacred sites. It has been rebuilt many times since it first covered the founder's body.

The 'little church of Columcille' that was seen by Magnús in 1098 may be represented by the *ante*, the projecting footings of local sandstone. These jut out near the ground, on either side of the little west door. These *ante* are a feature of early Irish churches where the stone emulated the original overhang of the preceding wooden church.

Only a handful of people could be in a church of this size at any one time, but it seems to have remained much the same throughout its life. It can be imagined as having the high walls and high pitched roof, as in the current rebuilding. This echoes the description of the stone church at Kells, perhaps the one completed in the year 816. The oldest church standing there is also to this design, on a larger scale.

In the Temptations scene in the *Book of Kells* (see p. 58) there is a church in the same simple style, with a high roof, with decorated gables. Here it is used to depict not only a church but the Ark of the Covenant, the Temple at Jerusalem and the Body of Christ. Perhaps all these meanings were associated with Saint Columba's shrine chapel, the place where his bodily resurrection would take place, even after his bones had been moved.

Perhaps this simple free-standing building was lime-washed white, as appears to have been the case with the original Saint Ronan's chapel. It must have stood out, for it was the centre of pilgrimage and the focus of the visitor's attention, marked (when it was standing) by Saint John's high cross. Pilgrims were allowed into the central site of the monastery, to pray at the tomb of the founder, sacred even when his remains had been removed to safety.

Excavations of the nearby pavement have shown that this area was rebuilt many times in later centuries. Each change still allowed access to the building and the integrity of this shrine chapel was preserved.

Under the floor, there are two stone cists. The remains of Columba and another person, perhaps one of the early abbots regarded as a saint, perhaps the body of Adomnán, may have once lain here.

The shrine chapel was the only building not levelled when the abbey was built for the Benedictine community.

During the later Middle Ages, the chapel ceased to be a separate building and became attached to the west wall of the abbey. Numerous graves were found close to its door. The pilgrim path around the abbey ended in this area.

During the centuries after the Reformation when it lay ruined, it was still pointed out to visitors as Saint Columba's shrine. It was rebuilt and fitted out in 1955. The tiny doorway reflects the low entrance to a previous church, and means that most adults have to stoop to enter.

Temptation of Christ page (folio 202v) from the Book of Kells.

Saint Columba's chapel, with the ante of an older building.

This century was a time of renewed writing in the Gaelic world. After the storms of the Viking age, and at a time of comparative safety, manuscripts were gathered, rewritten and developed.

We do not know whether this occurred on Iona, in a century of relative decline. People continued to visit, and pilgrims died here, and sometimes the gravestones were reused. Farming the land and fishing continued, to provide for visitors and for the community. The abbey seems to have retained its claim on various lands across the Hebrides, even in this period.

We can imagine the people living on the same regular, if monotonous, diet. Clothes were of wool, and perhaps of linen, both the end-product of intensive labour, mainly by women.

We may imagine a mixed community on the island, with residents of both sexes associated in some way with the monastery, and perhaps there was still a small community of ascetics.

Life was probably hard, but not necessarily unenjoyable, though it was precarious. Some seasons, like spring when the cows had dried up before calving, and 'hungry July' before the grain harvest, were always lean times. There must have been hard years when the weather yielded poor crops, when storms made travel, fishing and foraging the shores difficult.

One food was available fresh every spring, and a nutritious if hard-to-gather product all summer.

A prose gloss to the eighth-century poetical *Martyrology of Oengus* has this story about Saint Columba, which dates to the eleventh century. It may be intended to emphasize the kindness of the saint, or to make fun of overdoing austerity in emulating the extreme poverty that cannot sustain life. The tradition of Columba having a servant, with whom he was on close terms, goes back to Adomnán's *Life*.

Once when he was going round the graveyard in Iona, he saw an old woman cutting nettles for broth for herself. 'What is the cause of this, poor woman?' said Colum Cille. 'Dear Father,' said she, 'I have one cow and it has not yet borne a calf; I am waiting for it, and this is what has served me for a long time.' Colum Cille made up his mind then that nettle broth should be what should serve him mostly from then on for ever; saying, 'Since they suffer this great hunger in expectation of the one uncertain cow, it would be right for us that the hunger which we suffer should be great, waiting for God; because what we are expecting, the everlasting Kingdom, is better, and is certain.' And he said to his servant, 'Give me nettle broth every night,' said he, 'without butter or milk with it.' 'It shall be done,' said the cook. He hollowed the stick for stirring the broth and made it into a tube, so that he used to pour the milk into that tube and stir it into the broth. Then the people of the church noticed that the priest looked well, and talked of it among themselves. This was told to Colum Cille, and then he said, 'May your successors grumble for ever!' 'Now,' said he to the servant, 'what do you give me in the broth every day?' 'You yourself are witness,' said the menial, 'unless it comes out of the stick with which the broth is mixed, I know of nothing in it except broth alone.' Then the explanation was revealed to the priest, and he said, 'Prosperity and good deeds to your successor forever!' And this has come true.

(Jackson, 1971, pp. 296–7)

8

To 1203
The Winds of Change

Somewhere in Scotland, perhaps at Dunkeld, a certain Simeon wrote this prayer in Latin on a *Life of Saint Columba* copied for King Alexander I (1107–23). The poem plays on the word 'columba', both the saint's name and the word for 'dove'.

Holy Columba, our father, born of mother Ireland,
given by Christ's command to be the church's light,
may what we have written for you be pleasing to you, we pray.
For unworthily, yet lovingly, we have written down your deeds,
your life of virtue, heaven-adorned, we have set down.
We beseech you, through him ... forever
protect all those devoted to your service.
... and for everyone pour out your prayer ...

Be for the Scots a two-edged sword, be a mighty rampart,
and by your prayer bring goodness' help to Simeon your servant
who thought it fitting to write these words of prayer to you.
And William, who thought well to illuminate this book –
to him, O holy dove, impart your heavenly gifts.

(Clancy, 1998, pp. 185–6)

The saint was the protector of Scotland, with monasteries dedicated to Columba, though Iona itself remained part of the Norse political and religious world.

For this final long twelfth century of the Columban monastery, we know of several notable incidents. We also have some understanding of the buildings raised at that time, and can imagine the dramatic change from the cluster of small buildings to the larger structures of the later monastery.

Perhaps in the year 1100, the Columban foundation looked rather decayed, but it was not nearing its end. Later antiquarians and archaeologists saw the remnants of what they took to be stone cells where the abbey and cloister stand. There was also a rectangular stone church (Thomas, 1957, 1959, see *Argyll 4: Iona* p. 109).

Change in the way church life was organized was to come this century. The common early Christian practice in the Gaelic world had been to have bishops attached to monasteries. However, the normal practice in the wider Christian world was to have a bishopric that covered a defined geographical area. This form was to become established in the Gaelic world during this century.

The Kingdom of Man and the Isles had bishops of its own from the 1130s onwards. In 1152 the diocese was placed under the new archdiocese of Niðaróss, Trondheim in Norway. This massive archdiocese stretched from Norway across the Atlantic, taking in not only the Hebrides and Man, but Orkney and Shetland, the Faroe Islands, the two dioceses of Iceland and that of faraway Norse Greenland. In church terms, Iona, like the rest of the kingdom, was placed in the northern world, where Gaelic was not used, and the traditions of Ireland had no influence.

The new diocesan structure caused little change at first, but it was to position Iona both at the geographical edge of, yet firmly within, the universal Church with its centre in Rome.

In Ireland, change was coming too. There were three synods in the twelfth century, which led to the reform of ancient practices and created geographical dioceses on the same lines as on the Continent. In addition, in the middle of the century, Malachi of Armagh, a great reformer, visited Saint Bernard at Clairveaux, and on his return established the first Cistercian monastery in Ireland. Other continental orders were to follow.

Within the ancient monastic traditions, there was also change. The leader of the Columban monastic houses, Flaithbertach Ó Brolacháin, wanted to retain the ancient monastic lifestyle, but to reform it from within. He had already moved the headship of the Columban houses from Kells to Derry when another possibility emerged.

In 1164 a move was made to re-establish Iona as the leading house of the 'family' of Columban monasteries and to have the abbot, the successor of Columba, based here again. This proposal was supported by Somerled, King of the Isles, but was opposed by powerful figures within Ireland, and by the Scottish Crown. It came to nothing when Somerled was killed later that year.

The proposal is reported in the *Annals of Ulster*, and we get a glimpse into the monastic life on Iona at that time. It seems to have been going strong, for those consulted belonged to the main community; to a community of the ascetic Celí Dé, presumably living at Clàdh an Disert; and there was also a hermit.

After the 1164 proposal, a Domnall Ó Brolacháin from Derry was made abbot on Iona. It may have been the same Domnall whose death on 27 April 1203 in his old age, led to a much greater change with the refounding of the monastery as Benedictine.

In the meantime, from 1169 onwards, Ireland was convulsed by the arrival of the Anglo-Normans. After the initial violence of conquest was over, they too wished to show their piety and to claim continuity with the practices of the past. In 1185 the new Norman ruler of north-east Ireland, John de Courcy, claimed to have found Saint Columba's body, together with those of Saints Patrick and Bridget, at Downpatrick.

On Iona, meanwhile, the old monastic form of life continued. Perhaps towards the end of the century, the Augustinian nunnery was erected with the support of the family of Somerled. Building work also took place at the Reilig Oran.

Reilig Oran chapel

This plain but beautiful chapel, built for use by laypeople, is a link between the Columban abbey and the medieval Benedictine foundation. It may be built upon the site of a much older chapel, but can be considered the oldest building standing on the island, though it was ruined until rebuilt in 1957.

The surrounding burial ground, Reilig Odhráin, is the cemetery of Odhrán, Oran, who is said to have been a companion of Columba. Though he is not listed among the original twelve who left Ireland with Columba, there is evidence of an early cult of a saint of this name. In the eleventh-century *Life of Saint Columba*, in a story with only one parallel in Gaelic saints' *Lives*, Columba asks for a volunteer to die, to give the community roots on the island, to consecrate it. Oran, by now one of the original companions, volunteers, dies and goes to heaven.

An early thirteenth-century lament about Iona, the raids upon it and the change to the Benedictine rule, speaks of Reilig Oran as a much-loved place. The poet says that he used to go sunwise around it early every morning, to be freed from the burden of sin (Clancy, 1998, p. 245).

The chapel is a simple oblong building with a high-pitched roof and a door at the west end, very much in the Irish style. The style of this building is simple, very much like a larger version of a shrine chapel, and comparable with the high-pitched chapel at Kells.

The building may have replaced an older one, a mortuary chapel in the burial ground. The base of the current building may be as old as the earlier twelfth century one, and perhaps had a trabeate doorway, one with a lintel and stone jambs with a slope towards the ground.

It may then have been embellished in the mid-twelfth century, to add this distinctive rounded doorway in the Irish fashion of the time with its toothed decoration.

There is no east window, but two small windows, one on each side, give light to the altar area. What most visitors note is the quality of the sound, as the human voice echoes around the walls.

Although built by the powerful, it was used by all.

The chapel appears to be built as a mortuary chapel, for use at the funerals of secular rulers, probably those of the Kings of Man and the Isles. Guðröðr, King of Man was buried on Iona in 1188.

Before that time, most of the Hebrides had come by conquest in 1156 into the hands of his brother-in-law Somerled, ruler of Argyll. Although he was buried at the Cistercian monastery he founded at Saddell on Kintyre, Somerled may have had the building adapted to make it part of his domain, perhaps by adding the arched Romanesque doorway.

The family of Somerled and their successors, the Lords of the Isles, continued to use the chapel. In the floor are carved stones that cover the burials of the wealthy.

Others of the family were buried outside, and their stones have been brought under cover to preserve them, some of them mounted along the walls. These are the stones of male leaders. Perhaps the women were buried nearby at the nunnery.

On the south wall is the canopy of a tomb that has since vanished. It dates from the fifteenth century, well into the Benedictine period, and was perhaps designed at the same time the abbey was being rebuilt. The tomb may have been that of the last Lord of the Isles, John, who died in 1503 (photo, p. 73). There are carvings on the canopy, a crucifixion at the apex, the highest point. Here, the clothed Christ faces the onlooker, his arms wide in embrace, as on the MacLean cross (pp. 107–8). On the third arch down, at the apex, is a small, and now much weathered 'green man', a male face with foliage coming from the mouth.

Beside the door on the outside is a shelf-like cavity that was made in later times.

The cobbled 'Street of the Dead' passed just beside the west door. Oran's cross may have stood where the current wall cuts across the street, and where the large ditch and dike of the Columban *vallum* one stood, with a gateway for people to pass through.

This chapel stands as close as possible for the secular rulers to come to the sacred monastic space of the monastery. Here they are under the protection of Saint Columba and Saint Oran, at what was

Saint Oran's chapel in the Reilig Odhráin burial ground.

one of the ancient sites of the monastery. Their wealthy ancestors and other rulers lie nearby. So do the bones of unknown people.

The chapel continued in use throughout the medieval period, and into modern times. The burial ground gave space to seamen killed in the nineteenth century when their ship was wrecked off the west coast *machair*, and their grave is marked by an obelisk. An unknown sailor of the Second World War was buried here near the entrance gate. More recently the politician John Smith was buried in the extension area, under a large sea-washed stone. Following the traditional custom, his body lay overnight in the mortuary chapel the night before his funeral. Reilig Oran is still the islanders' burial ground.

The long-roofless Reilig Oran chapel is currently used as a place of private reflection in the daytime and sometimes for informal services. Requests can be left by a cross in the corner, to be read at the weekly service of prayers for healing in the abbey church.

The Communion table light is maintained by the Iona Community staff.

This twelfth-century poem in Irish is put in the mouth of Saint Columba.

Delightful I think it to be in the bosom of an isle
on the crest of a rock,
that I may look there on the manifold
face of the sea.

That I may see its heavy waves
over the glittering ocean
as they chant a melody to their Father
on their eternal course.

That I may see the smooth strand of clear headlands,
no gloomy thing;
that I may hear the voice of the wondrous birds,
a joyful course.

That I may hear the sound of the shallow waves
against the rocks;
that I may hear the cry beside the churchyard,
the roar of the sea.

That I may see its splendid flocks of birds
over the full-watered ocean;
that I may see its mighty whales,
greatest of wonders.

That I may see its ebb and its flood-tide
in its flow;
that this should be my name, a secret I declare,
'He who turned his back on Ireland'.

That contrition of heart should come upon me
when I look on it;
that I may bewail my many sins
difficult to declare.

That I may bless the Lord
who has power over all,
heaven with its crystal orders of angels,
earth, ebb, flood tide.

That I may pore on one of my books,
good for my soul,
a while kneeling for beloved heaven,
a while at psalms.

A while meditating upon the Prince of Heaven;
holy is the redemption,
a while at labour not too heavy;
it would be delightful!

A while gathering dilisk from the rock,
a while fishing,
a while giving food to the poor,
a while in my cell.

The counsel which is best before God
may He confirm it to me,
may the King, whose servant I am, not desert me,
May he not deceive me.

(Jackson, 1935, pp. 9–10)

A very similar text is provided by Jackson in his later *Celtic Miscel-lany*, pp. 279–80, but without the final verse. Dilisk, also called dulse, is an edible seaweed.

PART TWO

Medieval Iona

This part of the book is intended for use while visiting the medieval abbey and the nunnery, the sites which the poet William Wordsworth called the 'Glory of the West'.

The nunnery, abbey church and cloisters are never closed, nor is the Reilig Oran chapel. The rebuilt abbey's domestic buildings are occupied by staff and guests of the Iona Community, and are not open to the public.

The background

The rebuilt Benedictine abbey we see today is a replacement for the early Christian monastery founded on this site. The nearby Augustinian nunnery is also a medieval foundation. These continental orders were extremely popular in the Middle Ages and replaced early Christian monasteries in much of Ireland and Gaelic Scotland.

The way of life continued the existing monastic tradition and probably did not vary from it greatly.

Although the founding of the Benedictine abbey was controversial, pilgrimage continued to flourish. The monastery fell into unsavoury and disruptive circumstances in the later Middle Ages, but was strong enough to engage in extensive rebuilding in the fifteenth century. The nunnery was also partly rebuilt and extended at this time. At the sixteenth-century Reformation, monastery and nunnery were disbanded, but the existing monks and nuns were allowed to continue living in the premises, and received a pension.

Iona falls out of the Irish Annals after it became Benedictine in 1203. Ireland in the late twelfth century was itself going through convulsions with the invasion of Anglo-Normans, who conquered much of the island.

Even so, the original building shows Irish influence, as does the fifteenth-century rebuilding of much of the church and cloister, which reused many of the older stones. The same influence in the original building and the fifteenth-century rebuilding is seen in the nunnery.

The Kingdom and Bishopric of Man and the Isles (the Isle of Man and the Hebrides) had become part of the Church Province of Niðaróss, now Trondheim, in Norway in 1153.

The kings of Scotland were buried on Iona until the end of the eleventh century, and Scotland continued to have influence, as many of the rulers of the Isles also had land in mainland Scotland.

Politically, in the eleventh century, the Kingdom of Man and the Isles was subject to Norway, but in practice, like the archdiocese, the Kingdom of Norway usually had little impact, and local rule prevailed.

The Kingdom of Man and the Isles was divided in 1156, with the part in which Iona lies coming under the control of the family of Somerled (modern Gaelic Somhairle, Norse Sumarliði), ruler of Argyll. This family, which also possessed land on the mainland that was subject to Scotland, gave the title 'king' to all those in the male line who descended from Somerled. One of Somerled's sons, named Ragnall (Norse Rögnvaldr, Latin Reginaldus), is credited with the re-founding of the monastery of Iona.

Norway sold the Kingdom of Man and the Isles to Scotland in 1265. The Kings of the Isles' descendants became known as the Lords of the Isles, and many of the sculpted gravestones on the island commemorate members of this family.

Special powers had been given to Iona in relation to the Bishopric of Man and the Isles. Then, during the fourteenth century, England gained firm control over the Isle of Man, and in effect the diocese split in two. The bishopric remained part of the Norwegian archdiocese until 1472, when it became part of the Scottish church. After the Reformation in the seventeenth century, there was a short-lived attempt to restore the chancel of Iona abbey to make it the cathedral.

The Lordship of the Isles was forfeited to the Scots Crown in 1493.

Saint Oran's chapel: tomb canopy for one of the later Lords of the Isles, perhaps the last, John Macdonald, who died in 1503.

After the Reformation of the mid-sixteenth century the abbey and nunnery slowly fell into ruins. The abbey's domestic buildings were rebuilt during the middle of the twentieth century by the Iona Community, an ecumenical Christian community founded by George MacLeod and others in 1938.

The Community received summer guests from the start, and this practice continues today, with weekly guests, who often follow a specific programme. The staff employed by the Community also organize the daily worship services, at 9 am, 9 pm, and during the summer months at 2 pm, all of which are open to the public.

9

The Benedictine Abbey

The abbey is built largely of local pink granite, with limestone from Mull for the dressed, carved stonework, and some Mull sandstone as well.

The west door

The west door of the abbey church, dedicated to Saint Mary and Saint Columba, lies near the earlier high crosses, the Columba chapel, and the later well. Entering the building, we meet the work of many centuries, of prayer and of rebuilding during the 900 years that the walls have stood.

Entering the abbey from the west door gives a sense of the building, which sweeps downward to the focal point, the Communion table under the east window.

This abbey is built upon the site of the earlier churches of the Columban monastery. Raised at a time when most people had little experience of large stone buildings, it served the monastic community and its visitors for 350 years, and as the islanders' church for another two centuries. It was rebuilt 100 years ago and is today again a place of daily Christian worship. What we see from the west door is largely the church as it was rebuilt in the fifteenth century and restored and furnished in the twentieth.

The crossing

To explore the different layers in this building, and what they meant to people of their time, it is helpful to move down the first part of the church, the nave (from Latin *navis*, ship, one of the images for church in the sense of people) to the crossing, the place where the two wings of the church jut out at each side, under the central tower.

The original church was erected very early in the thirteenth century. It seems to have been raised in a hurry and the walls are thin in places. The only remaining parts are the north wall, which is to the left when facing the Communion table. In the nave this probably means most of the existing wall. In the choir, the part nearer the front of the church, we can follow the string course, the line of decorated stone standing out from the wall. This stops some way before the arches with their opening to the choir loft. The original east end with window and altar would have stood here.

The original stone church was narrower than the present one by about a metre. Underneath it were the remains of a small rectangular church. The abbey church was extended eastward to a new high altar only about 20 years after being built, to accommodate the number of visiting pilgrims.

This church, and the later extensions, would have looked very different from the plain stone that attracts us today. The walls can be imagined as plastered inside and then painted with biblical scenes and similar devotional art, accompanied by colourful statues.

The choir was used by the choir-monks, whose main work was to sing the Office, the psalms and associated chants, and to attend the other liturgies, in particular Masses. The nave was used by laybrothers, members of the monastic community who had less rigorous duties in church but worked the land and provided for pilgrims; and by laypeople, islanders and visiting pilgrims.

Also part of the very early church is the north transept, which is entered from the crossing. To understand the building, we may consider what happened in 1203–04.

The monastery founded by Saint Columba had continued to live to the ancient early Christian monastic way of life for some 650 years. We do not know, then or later, how large the community was, but the site was a revered place for pilgrims to visit, and the community maintained its ties with Ireland and the Columban monasteries there. Whether change was planned or not, in the end it came rapidly.

On 27 April 1203 the elderly abbot Domnall died. On 9 December 1203 Pope Innocent III signed a charter to Celestinus (Cellach), abbot of Saint Columba, Iona, allowing him to establish a Benedictine monastery. He names the lifestyle of the monks, and gives protection from all secular powers, and from the need to pay tithes or to be subject to the bishop. The lands already belonging to the monastery and now part of the Benedictine establishment included those on Iona, Mull, Tiree, Islay, Colonsay, Oransay, Canna, and others that cannot always be identified (Goss, pp. 153–4).

This change did not go unchallenged. Although the monastery at Derry had been devastated by fire in 1204, the *Annals of Ulster* report that same year:

A monastery was built by Cellach, abbot of Iona in the centre of the enclosure of Iona, without any right, in dishonour of the Community of Iona, so that he wrecked the place greatly. A hosting, however, was made by the clergy of Ireland [bishops and abbots are named], and a large number of the Community of Doire [Derry] and a large number of the clergy of the North, so that they razed the monastery, according to the law of the Church. That Amalgaidh aforesaid took the abbacy of Iona by selection of Foreigners [Anglo-Normans] and Gaidhil [native Irish].

The building, however, continued apace and were it not for these records we might think from the style that it had started some time earlier. It is likely that the older community was not expelled nor was there an influx of new monks, but that the Benedictine rule was adopted by the majority of the community, and had long been planned. Perhaps a dissenting minority had reported the event to the head of the Columban *familia* at Derry.

The new monastery was supported by Ragnall son of Somerled, a powerful King of the Isles, who died in about 1207. He seems to have kept the peace in his lifetime, but shortly afterwards Derry was pillaged twice by his sons, perhaps in revenge. There is a poem in Gaelic from about 1210 which laments the arrival of 'foreign monks', though this might mean native monks adhering to the new rule (Clancy, 1998, pp. 242–6). The new site was also pillaged by a band of Norwegians in 1210.

This background explains something of why the monastery is where it is, and why the monastic church had a cloister built on the north side, rather than undertaking the more conventional but slower work of diverting the watercourse to allow a cloister with a warmer southern aspect. The monastery deliberately covers the sacred land of the older Columban centre, except the shrine chapel of Saint Columba himself.

As the *Annals of Ulster* state, and the archaeology indicates, the building started right in the middle of the site. It was not necessary to build here: there was plenty of land nearby, though it might have meant razing other structures or disturbing graves. The monks could have built the monastic church to the west of where it stands, incorporating the shrine chapel into an apse behind the high altar, or in some other prominent position nearby. It seems that the Benedictines wanted to claim the central sacred space, to be seen as the successors of Columba, even if it meant building rapidly. The structures of the Columban monastery were razed, the stones perhaps reused in the abbey walls, providing a continuity of its own.

The north transept

We enter the north transept through a rebuilt arch, under a scene carved in the later Middle Ages of Adam and Eve in the Garden of Eden. This reminder of human origins and of the Fall and redemption reaches its high point in the Eucharist celebrated at the east end of the church.

This transept is part of the oldest church, with the original floor level. It is designed in a conservative style, more reminiscent of the twelfth than the thirteenth century. Perhaps the building of the Benedictine abbey had long been discussed and architect's plans drawn up some time earlier.

There are two small windows, which once provided the light from the east. One now has the twentieth-century stained-glass image of Columba, designed by William Wilson in 1965. Beneath the windows are the stone bases of two small altars. Many of the choir monks were ordained priests, and their duties required the saying of a daily Mass. Small altars were used, often at the sides of churches, to enable this to take place at the same time. Between the windows is an arched recess of Romanesque Irish-style architecture.

About 20 years after this wall was built, the light was blocked when an aisle to what is now the choir loft was made, in the first restructuring of the church. Later, in the fifteenth century, the windows were unblocked again.

Above in the north wall can be seen the edge of what is a passage set in the wall. This is one of several passages that allowed for maintenance higher in the building. Often they appeared at clerestory level, the level on which large windows were found, but here they are in the blank wall.

The ceiling is high and of stone, not wood. The original church appeared to have had a high roof, which shows something of the skill of the architects. In the north-east corner is one of the shafts intended to carry a ribbed vault, but it was never completed.

There is also a rose window in the north wall, near the top. This was designed by James Honeyman and dates to 1904. The upper wall was too damaged to have retained any such feature from the Middle Ages. The rebuilding of the domestic buildings meant that the natural light to this window was blocked off.

In the south wall are two windows. The door to the cloister was part of a later rebuild.

Rose window, from inside.

This northern transept was first built unattached to any buildings except the church. But once the cloister was added on this side of the church, it was necessary to build night stairs from the monks' dormitories, which were used when they attended the night Offices, the chanting of psalms and other prayers in the middle of the night. The current stone steps leading to the residential part of the abbey buildings replicate the night stairs.

Coming down to night prayers, and returning to their beds afterwards for the second period of sleep, the Benedictine monks had the encouragement of being blessed. In the arch between the two windows on the north wall, the feet of a statue can be seen. The length of the ankle suggests a male figure. It is probably Saint Columba giving his blessing and protection to the abbey and to their prayer. The figure and surrounding arch will be seen again in the church.

Perhaps the unused base of the arch for the roof at times held a statue, perhaps of the Virgin Mary blessing the monks as they returned to bed. There was another arch base on the north-west side, which may have also been reused from time to time.

The oak rood screen that divides this transept from the main church is modern, a gift from Queen Elizabeth in 1956.

For many years this part of the abbey had exhibitions relating to the social justice work of the Iona Community.

The chancel

Moving into the chancel brings us to a complex array of building through the ages.

The oldest aspects are not all visible. Looking up to where the wall of the chancel meets the crossing, a projecting stone can be seen. This is at the end of a short corridor within the wall. In its ceiling, at the base of the wall holding up the tower, is a quern stone, a circular stone used for grinding corn. Taken from the earlier monastery after it was too worn for use, it was reused to hold up the tower. The projecting stone at the end of this corridor, which is now used for electrical wiring, may once have held a statue.

The pillars of the crossing are gouged on the chancel side. During the 1630s, during the brief attempt to make this building the cathedral of the Isles, the chancel was partitioned off. The crossing was made into a chamber, while the nave was abandoned. This attempt did not last, but some of the marks can be seen in the fabric, examples of how people have sought new uses for this place over the centuries.

Within a few years of the church being built at the start of the thirteenth century, the decision was made to extend it eastwards. The floor was raised substantially, while the east wall was pulled down and a new one built in what is now the presbytery (the raised area around the Communion table). The south choir with its graceful arches was built at what was the new level of the floor. The space below made an undercroft, perhaps used to store relics. In the north transept the windows were blocked from the light by the new south aisle.

The arches are carved with toothed ornament similar to the rounded arches of the chapter house (p. 99). Here, they have the graceful point which had become normal at the time. Once, a carved head looked out from where the arches meet, perhaps representing Saint Benedict. The arches were later blocked, though their outline was retained (as were the arches at the nunnery, page 114), and the floor restored to the level we see today.

In the choir loft, the east window has a pointed hood and a style very similar to the nunnery's south chapel window.

This part of the building is now a sacristy and the music loft, from where a piano and other instruments are played during services.

Mouth of the dumb,	Os mutorum,
light of the blind,	lux cecorum,
foot of the lame,	pes clausorem,
to the fallen	porrige
stretch out your hand.	Lapsis manum,
Strengthen the senseless,	Firma vanum
restore the mad.	et insanum corrige.
O Columba, hope of Scots,	O Columba spes Scotorum
by your merits' mediation,	nos tuorum meritorum
make us companions	interventu beatorum
of the blessed angels.	fac consortes angelorum.
Alleluia.	Alleluia.

From the fourteenth-century *Inchcolm Antiphoner* (Broun and Clancy, 1999; also Clancy, 1998, p. 318)

During the rebuilding in the fifteenth century and the lowering of the floor to its original level, a finely carved new doorway was inserted below the arches. At this time too, the building connecting this aisle to the north transept was taken down and the windows there again received some natural daylight.

Saint Brigit's window.

Above the arches, three glass windows were inserted during the rebuilding of the early twentieth century. Nearest the east is the earliest saint, Patrick, then Bridget, then Columba. Opposite, the easternmost window depicts the eleventh-century Queen Margaret of Scotland, who helped to restore the Columban monastery.

The choir, where the monks sang during the offices, would have been divided from the nave and crossing by a wooden rood screen, decorated with carvings of saints painted in bright colours like the walls which are now bare of plaster.

The fixed wooden pews were added when the church was restored in the early twentieth century. They replicate the style of choir seats in medieval churches, which faced inwards so that people on each side could sing the psalms antiphonally; taking turns to sing a verse. The reading desk at the crossing also dates from the modern period, and is now used for leading the liturgy, and for preaching, replacing the wooden pulpit, which was also made at that time.

The presbytery

This is the focus of the church, of the architecture and of people's prayer. It is raised, set apart from the main body of the church.

This part was rebuilt in the fifteenth century, probably under the master mason Domnall Ó Brolacháin, who came from a Derry family. There is a large central window, and another at each side. Some of the carvings that embellished them remain. On the south presbytery window at the spring of the arch, there is on one side a cat (with an oak-leaf tail) and on the other a monkey.

Presbytery, cat carving by the window.

The three large windows bring light to the high altar where the Communion table now stands. This faced east, towards the rising sun and Jerusalem, a constant reminder of the resurrection while the sacrifice of the Last Supper, the Garden and Calvary were re-enacted here.

The contemporary Communion table is made of Iona marble, as was the original, which was chipped away by souvenir hunters in the eighteenth century. In the Middle Ages, a painted crucifix would have stood here: the ring-headed silver cross is a twentieth-century work.

The oldest Gospel tells of the Last Supper in this way:

While they were eating, Jesus took bread, and when he had given thanks, he broke it and gave it to his disciples, saying, 'Take it; this is my body.' Then he took a cup, and when he had given thanks, he gave it to them, and they all drank from it. 'This is my blood of the covenant, which is poured out for many,' he said to them. 'Truly I tell you, I will not drink again from the fruit of the vine until that day when I drink it new in the kingdom of God.' When they had sung a hymn, they went out to the Mount of Olives.

(Mark 14.22–26)

Under the south window are three seats, divided by small pillars, and accompanied by carved heads which are now very worn, or have been replaced. This is the *sedilla*, the place where those leading the liturgy could sit. The structure of the *sedilla* is designed to give out an echo that amplifies the voice, and enabled the leader to be heard by the monks chanting with him.

Also here are two stone effigies of former abbots, both originally raised impressively upon pedestals. The more weathered figure under the *sedilla* probably commemorates the fifteenth-century Abbot Dominic. He lies in state, but at his feet crawls an enormous toad. The other figure, also in liturgical dress, commemorates Abbot John MacKinnon. The inscription indicates that he had this effigy prepared with the intention of living into the sixteenth century, but he died short of it in 1498. His mitre has a bat on

Presbytery, restored carving on sedilia *bracket.*

it, perhaps a memento mori, a reminder that we all face death in the end. Both effigies suffered indignity from theft and vandalism: the last attempt to steal John MacKinnon's head was during the rebuilding of the abbey.

As with the other dead of the community, they would originally have been included in the life of prayer, as they had died and come before God. The hope was that each fellow monk would soon after death enter heaven and become part of the choir of the communion of saints. They could then intercede directly with God for those still on earth. They provided a link in ongoing prayer to the founder Columba.

In the centre of the floor, and once outlined in brass, is another figure, a long-forgotten secular ruler.

The bones of many others were found during the restoration work in the early twentieth century, and the places have been marked with small lead crosses set in the floor. Some of those in the chancel and nave (where the laybrothers were probably buried) were accompanied by a number of pebbles. These possibly tallied with the number of years the monk had been in religious life, and these can be seen fixed in the floor. White pebbles from the beach were also found with the later burials in St Ronan's church, and are commonly found in Ireland and western Scotland.

South chapel, south aisle and pillars

This was once entered by an elaborate arch, the footings of which are under one of the grills that mark where there are older architectural remnants under the current floor level.

This area has a window looking east and would have housed one or more of the additional monastic altars. There is also a south-facing window. This area was a favourite place for prayer, even during the centuries of ruin, and remains a place for private reflection. Many people leave prayers on the cross and net, and requests left in a box on the south window are included each week in the Iona Community's Tuesday night service for healing.

The south aisle in its present form dates to the fifteenth-century rebuilding. An attempt had been made in the thirteenth century to build a large south transept to the abbey church, to accommodate pilgrims. There was to be a room above, reached by a winding stair. The plan never got beyond the foundation level, and much later this south aisle was built. It incorporates an attempt to buttress the southern wall with its two semicircular arches, while a larger arch leads into the north transept.

This rather dark area with small windows now houses displays on the social justice commitments of the Iona Community. They form a passage to the place for quiet prayer.

The pillars

The pillars hold up the pointed arches of this side of the chancel. Their capitals, the decorated upper parts of these pillars, were carved during the fifteenth-century rebuilding of the abbey. Oak leaves abound here, as on many pillars around the abbey, a reminder of the links with Derry, the 'oak grove', its links to Saint Columba, which was also the home of the master mason Domnall Ó Brolacháin. Many of the carvings have survived through the centuries when the roof was open, though some have suffered water damage.

While they are hard to see because of the choir stalls, the south pillars have much to tell. The carver used them to make links with older carvings on the site, and to give new insights.

The easternmost pillar, closest to the high altar, covers aristocratic and largely secular themes. There is foliage and interlace. In one scene a man on a horse and another on foot have their backs to the altar area while they engage

East pillar carvings.

in warfare or hunting. Two lions confront each other, their necks entwined. Facing the south aisle is a slender pelican-like bird, facing a much larger griffins beak to beak, while a dragon-like creature looks on and shoots more foliage from its jaws.

A different life is depicted in the middle pier. On the side facing into the body of the church, at an angle that points to the north transept, is the figure of a man in liturgical dress, wearing a mitre. He holds in his left hand an old Irish crozier, with a curved end like a modern walking stick. His right hand is held up in blessing. This must be Saint Columba. The frame around the figure and the direction in which the figure is turned, towards the north transept, makes it likely that it was a small replica of the statue that stood there, of which only the feet survive.

To the right of Columba is a crucifixion scene, with a fully clothed Jesus holding his arms out at right angles to his body. He is accompanied, as tradition expects, by the figures of Saint John and the centurion Longinus.

Central pillar carvings.

This is, however, not only the crucified but also the resurrection Jesus, walking towards the people to embrace and protect them. A small hump may represent either the hill of Calvary or the shrine chapel of Saint Columba outside the west end of the abbey.

Following the arch round (by moving around the end of the fixed choir stalls and into the south aisle), there can next be seen Mary, holding out the child Jesus towards the brothers and lay-people in the nave. She too is in an arch, perhaps one made of a scroll held by the angels, one on either side of her. It seems that the figure of Jesus is turning outwards to bless the people. Although there are only two angels here, Jesus holds the same posture as on Saint Martin's cross, while on Saint Oran's cross (which was perhaps already fallen), Jesus leans towards his mother. The Virgin Mary took precedence in heaven, even to Columba: indeed later writers thought that the abbey like the nunnery was dedicated to her. Here, she is on one side of Christ, and Columba is on the other.

Further round the pillar, on the side nearer to the presbytery, the place where Christ's sacrifice and redemption are recalled, there are other scenes. Three figures appear to be beating a central figure which holds a staff but does not defend himself. This seems to be Christ during his Passion, holding the staff of office but not exercising his power.

In the final scene, an angel with a sword holds out the scales of judgement on which at our death our sins and good deeds are weighed. The angel looks not at the scales but backwards towards Columba for guidance. Meanwhile, a fierce beast is trying to hold down one side, to bring the scales down on the side of damnation, but is distracted by a bird that stands on its back and pecks at its bottom.

This long-necked and long-legged bird has the outline of a crane, the bird associated with Columba. As a crane forages for food with its beak, so does this bird, its wing feathers curled behind, giving the impression of a large rump.

Columba is present, as abbot and guide, at our judgement, and is on the side of the sinner under his protection.

The carving has no beginning or end but is a continuous sequence, like the yearly cycle of prayer. Christ's ever-present sacrifice and return, the blessing and protection of Mary and Columba, and prayers to them, will help in the time of trial, taking the burden of the weight of sin at the judgement.

The carvings of the westernmost pillar, closest to where laybrothers and visitors stood, are connected by a weathered string course, and merge with those of the north chancel arches and the choir arch. If the easternmost pillar of the south aisle has an aristocratic and secular theme, this group displays matters that relate to the lives of the other classes.

There is a fantastic beast entwined upon itself, and a man pulling at a bull. There is the Garden of Eden of our first parents, Adam and Eve, with the tree, the snake and the angel holding aloft a sword at their expulsion. There is a scene where a cow is taken from a begging figure and seems about to be slaughtered. The

West pillar carvings.

figures are all in contemporary clothing and the scene no doubt relates to contemporary concerns in a society where cattle were very important as a source of food and wealth. The scene may refer also to the many stories about Columba providing and protecting the cows of the poor; and especially the account of the theft of Columba's own cow from which he gave his cats milk. Two leaping creatures, perhaps cats, accompany the cow in this scene.

There are interlocked beasts, the strange head of a Neptune-like figure and perhaps a sea serpent. A fierce bearded figure looks out, with a lion on each side of his head. On one pillar, facing the chancel crossing and below the main decoration, the faint outline of a serene angel can be seen, hands folded, knees bent as if just alighted. In small capitals and recorded before part broke away, are the words: 'Donaldus O Brolacháin *fecit hic opus*', Domnall Ó Brolacháin made this work.

Between the activities and symbols of the upper classes and the day-to-day life of the farming and fishing community, the central pillar speaks of the focus of the monastic life. It provides a calm centre of prayer for one's own salvation, and that of the world around. The scenes depicted are of the circle of redemption, while the activities on the pillars on each side are occurring simultaneously to the timeless images on this central pillar. The monk's life is to achieve salvation by the life of prayer. This cycle is not apart from the world, but seeks the centre, Christ's presence through the incarnation and redemption in every aspect of life.

The themes of the pillars unify past and present, the Benedictine and the Columban. The Eden scene was on the Matthew cross outside the west door, the Columba carving referred to what may have been a statue in the north transept chapel, and the scenes in contemporary dress may have referred both to current events and the stories told about Columba. Perhaps there were other sculpted and plaster representations that Domnall and his school made to echo those on these pillars.

I pray you, Christ, to change my heart
To make it whole;
Once you took on flesh like mine,
Now take my soul.

Ignominy and pain you knew,
The lash, the scourge,
You, the perfect molten metal
Of my darkened forge.

You make the bright sun bless my head,
Put ice beneath my feet,
Send salmon leaping in the tides,
Give crops of wheat.

When Eve's wild children come to you
With prayerful words,
You crowd the rivers with fine fish,
The sky with birds.

You make the small flowers thrive
In the wholesome air,
You spread sweetness through the world
What miracle can compare?

> Irish, by Tadghd Óg Ó hUiginn (d. 1448), translated by
> Brendan Kennelly (Murray, p. 29). A prose translation is by
> Jackson (1971, p. 300)

Through the south door

From the south aisle there is a door which leads outside. Leaving by this, we see the base of the large south aisle that was never built. Prayer and practicality meet, as the large drainage course is one of the parts that can seen.

Perhaps the plan was too ambitious, or too expensive. However, it was in the right place. In the field to the south-east, about 200 metres away, are the ruins of a small medieval church called Saint Mary's chapel. The original road the pilgrims took to the abbey passed by its west end. The road had come from the landing place, passed east of the nunnery and continued on what is now the tarmac road to MacLean's cross. It then passed straight through what are now the Columba Hotel gardens. This chapel, near to the line of the ancient monastic *vallum*, looks like a final stopping place for rest and prayer before entering the sacred precincts.

When pilgrims had passed the chapel they continued towards the east end of the abbey, to meet it below the south presbytery window. The fifteenth-century window is decorated on the inside, and also has weathered carved figures on the outside. Vivid and in high relief, possibly once painted, these are the sights that greeted the pilgrims as they made their final journey to the church.

The figure at the top of the arched window seems have hands raised towards heaven. Below are two figures, the one on the left apparently male. He is naked to the ribs, lolls sideways, and has his tongue extended. The figure on the right is slenderer and has her head covered. One long hand rests on the knee and she also leans sideways. These two figures may represent pilgrims, depicted at the hour of their death. In the hour of their need, as they come to judgement, the topmost figure, Columba, intercedes to heaven for them. Having honoured him by pilgrimage in life, and having supported the upkeep of his sacred site, they will be under his protection wherever they may die.

Having encountered these images, the pilgrims then passed round the south side of the church, where the large south aisle was once planned for their accommodation. They then walked round to the west end to the high crosses, and to take their turn entering the tiny relic chapel of Saint Columba, queuing perhaps as pilgrims queue today to enter the Holy Sepulchre's tomb in Jerusalem. The pilgrims could then enter through the west door of the abbey church, to look down its length and to the light-filled presbytery with the high altar that faced Jerusalem.

South presbytery window.

The crossing and tower

Returning inside, we turn to the centre of the abbey church. Above is the central tower, with three floors. One was the belfry, with a bell that is rung for services. Another is a dovecot. Doves were part of medieval life, as they produced eggs, feathers for bedding, and fertilizer. They were a reminder that Columba is the Latin word for dove.

The crossing of the church has arches of different ages on all four sides. In the north chancel arch the outline of the older, higher, arch can be seen. The footings can also be seen at floor level.

The arch that leads into the nave was rebuilt in the fifteenth century, when the nave was widened about a metre on the south side. High on this arch there is a solitary human face carved in high relief, a soul in distress. While the plaster paintings of the past may not have made it seem as isolated as it is now, it is possible that the face represents the human condition, the need for solace and guidance from hearing the preached word. For a modern speaker centred in the crossing, it can serve as a focus for directing the voice, to ensure that it can be heard throughout the abbey.

Another kind of carving occupies the arch to the south transept, where monkeys play.

The south transept

The south transept is part of the original early thirteenth-century church, though it is much changed. It is now blocked by an iron grill and contains two marble effigies made in 1908. One is of the eighth Duke of Argyll, while the other is of his third wife Ina, who was buried here. The grill and these marble figures occupy the entire south transept in a manner not unusual for their time.

The Duke arranged for the consolidation of the abbey ruins in 1874–75, and many features were recorded. Then, in 1899, he bequeathed the lands on which the ruined abbey and nunnery stood to a Trust, an action that enabled the abbey church to be rebuilt between 1902 and 1914. A copy of the Charter is framed on the wall.

The Duke was ahead of his time, and in spite of opposition from his own Church of Scotland minister, he insisted that the abbey would be open to worship for all Christian denominations. Shortly before, the Episcopalians had built the retreat house nearby. In the Scotland of the time, opening the abbey to Catholics was controversial.

The Duke died in 1900, long before the plans for the modern use of the restored buildings had been made. Although the grilled area takes up space that often is needed, the actions of this couple led to the foundation of the Iona Community, to complete the work by rebuilding the domestic part of the abbey.

A reminder that others changed and restored the building, and have died centuries ago, is given by a mason's mark on the east wall.

Consecration cross in south transept.

The nave and west door

The north wall of the nave is part of the original building, while the south wall was completely rebuilt in the fifteenth century to broaden this part of the church.

The nave was the domain of the laybrothers, who did much of the physical, agricultural work of the abbey. They prayed, and were eventually buried here. Laypeople attended services from the nave as well. There were no furnishings – people stood or brought something to sit or kneel on. Doors on the north side allowed the laybrothers access to the private area of the monastery, the cloisters, while pilgrims entered by the west door, which was also the ceremonial door.

This part of the building needed the most restoration at the beginning of the twentieth century. Yet, although the abbey church decayed, and the roof fell in during the early eighteenth century, the island people came and prayed here on Sundays. Later, visitors with a sense of place, like the English travellers Johnson and Boswell, found themselves also moved to prayer here. Many also sketched it as it decayed, and these drawings helped with the rebuilding.

Much was done during the rebuilding to keep the style of a medieval church, though without the colourful plastering. The stone corbels holding up the roof are carved, as the originals would have been. Also, very much of the twentieth century is the book in the glass case, a record of the Benefactors.

The font is usually placed at the west end of the church, and signifies the place of entry to the Christian community.

> [After the resurrection] Jesus came to them and said, 'All authority in heaven and on earth has been given to me. Therefore go and make disciples of all nations, baptizing them in the name of the Father and of the Son and of the Holy Spirit, and teaching them to obey everything I have commanded you. And surely I am with you always, to the very end of the age.'
>
> (Matthew 28.18–20)

A medieval abbey did not perform baptisms: these occurred in the islanders' parish church. After the Reformation, when the monastic church became a secular one, a font must have been installed. The current one, which from time to time is used for baptisms, dates from 1913 and is partly made of Iona marble.

The small set of stairs in the corner of the nave leads to a cell-like room, created when Saint Columba's chapel was joined to the abbey in the fifteenth century. Later associated with Saint Oran, it has a low ceiling, a round form, and a small window that overlooks the high crosses. Perhaps this served to monitor the passage of pilgrims. It may also have provided additional altar space for the more supple priests among the monks. The small cupboard-like recess may have held the sacred vessels. The fern that grows here today is found also in the presbytery area.

Outside the west door

This area is dominated by the high crosses, the replica of Saint John's cross outside Saint Columba's chapel, the base where Saint Matthew's cross stood, and beyond it, Saint Martin's cross. Immediately outside the abbey, the pavement has been built and rebuilt many times. The well seems to have been made in the fifteenth century.

The stones that lie outside include a shallow trough with a cross carved at one end. Later tradition suggests it was used by pilgrims to wash their feet before entering Saint Columba's chapel. Another stone has three hollows incised in it. Perhaps these stones had a practical use to the builders. Other stones, now lost, were, according to visitors in the eighteenth century, used for swearing oaths.

The cobbled street, now called the Street of the Dead, is a medieval road that follows the track of a much older road through the Columban monastery. One part of it branched towards the west door, while the other continued and ended at the bake house, which is now a garden.

The cloisters

Turning back inside, we can enter the cloister from the church. This is the square arcade with the garden in the centre of the domestic buildings.

It was raised soon after the north wall and transept of the church were built. It was not part of the original plan – on the east side a clear line in the masonry distinguishes the outside of the north transept from the cloister building. The monks worked fast to build rather than divert the mill-stream, needed to provide fresh water and then to flush the latrines. Or perhaps there were other buildings to the south, or a cemetery, which they did not wish to disturb.

The cloister had a wide passage on each of its four sides, with a sloping roof. The side facing inwards was, as usual, arcaded, open to the air and held up by a series of narrow pillars ending in arches.

Although restructured in the 1400s, the rebuilt cloisters followed the design of the 1200s. Two of the original pillars still stand in the south-west corner. The modern replacements have mostly been carved by the sculptor Chris Hall and assistants between 1967 and 1997. They follow a distinct theme, in sequence on each side.

In the north-east corner of the cloisters, close to the church, the remains of an older building jut out into the cloister garden. The mass grave of very young men was found here in 1957. The Benedictines knew about the grave when they built this place for their relaxation and meditation, and they left this stonework to mark it.

The eastern side of the cloisters contains the Chapter House, which was first built early in the thirteenth century, and is now used again. From a large ante room we move through the two great Romanesque arches, which are carved much like the slightly later pointed arches in the church choir. In the inner room, the monks met daily to listen to a chapter of the Rule of Saint Benedict, and to discuss the community's work and business. Around the edges are alcoves from the later rebuilding phase, which provided seating. Above, there was a room, which may have been the library, as it is today.

It is possible after some evening services to visit the upstairs refectory, which is used by the Iona Community. This large room had a reading desk in one corner. The monks ate in silence while one of them read aloud.

Around the edges of the cloister, tombstones of West Highland carving are fixed to the walls. Many have a ship carved on them, a reminder that for centuries travel by sea was the norm, and the easiest way to get from place to place. The West Highlands became famous for their galleys, made from the great trees that grew in such places as the deep valleys of the Isle of Mull.

At the centre of the cloisters stands a twentieth-century sculpture, 'The Descent of the Spirit'. A dove holds a canopy pierced with stars, which cradles the figure of a young woman, whose arms are open to receive and to unite with it. Three angels are bringing the canopy to earth, where it is received by a lamb. The woman and the angels are as yet sightless: only the lamb has eyes.

This 1959 work is by the Lithuanian artist Jakob Lipchitz (1891–1973), who worked in Paris and had to flee the Nazi occupation. The inscription reads:

Jacob
Lipchitz
Juif fidèle
â la foi de ses ancêtres
a fait cette Vierge pour
la bonne entente des
hommes sur la terre afin
Que l'Esprit régne

(Jacob Lipchitz, a Jew faithful to the religion of his ancestors, has made this Virgin for the good understanding between the peoples of the earth, that the Spirit may reign)

Stories of why Columba went to Iona kept being told down the centuries, and many were collected in the long *Life*, compiled in 1532 at the behest of Mánus Ó Domhnaill (Manus O'Donnell), prince and scholar of a Donegal family that traced its roots back to Columba's people.

Mánus (c.1490–1563) was an innovative Renaissance man, who translated from the Latin sources, modernized the Irish ones, and used popular tradition, all to compile a chronological account of Columba's life. He was also insistent that the work be associated with his name, at a time when it was rare to claim authorship of prose works. This may explain in part why the most famous account of Columba's coming to Iona is first provided by Mánus.

In Mánus' account, Columba, while still in Ireland, borrowed a Psalter from Saint Finnian, and secretly copied it at night in the church.

On the final night, Finnian sent a boy to fetch the Psalter. The boy looked through a hole in the door and saw the book being copied by light coming from Columba's fingers. The saint became aware of the boy, and sent his pet crane to swoop down on the hole and pluck out the boy's eye. Fortunately, Saint Finnian healed him.

When Finnian received the original back at the end of Columba's visit, he demanded the copy made without his consent. Columba disputed this, as no harm had been done to the original, and the Word of God was to be spread.

The high king judged that, just as 'to every cow its calf, to every book its copy'. As a calf follows its mother cow, so a copy goes with its original. Columba continued to dispute this, and the matter became one of the reasons for the battle of Cúl Drebene in Sligo, at which many died.

Columba was told by the Archangel Michael that God would not abandon him and that his party would win the battle, but that Columba would have to do great penance and leave Ireland forever. When this was confirmed by another saint, Columba left his native land, in great grief.

The Psalter went with him, it seems, just as a full-grown calf is in time sold or given onwards. The story continues that it is the same Psalter that the O'Donnells carry in its shrine around their forces before battle, to ensure victory. The name given to it, *cathach*, means 'battler', in reference both to its spiritual value and later use.

A shrine for the Psalter was made in the Columban monastery at Kells during the late eleventh century, and in this the O'Donnells carried it. This was long kept unopened, which preserved the Psalter, one of the oldest of our manuscripts (O'Donnell, 1998, pp. 97–111).

Cranes are associated with Saint Columba in several stories. These attractive wading birds were common in Ireland until the seventeenth century. They are similar in outline to a heron (the same word, *corr*, is used for both in Irish), but they fly with their neck outstretched and at certain seasons gather in multitudes (Adomnán, 1991, note pp. 311–12).

Mánus Ó Domhnaill was writing nearly a 1,000 years after Columba, but in the time when the age of printing was still young. He intended to publish the compilation under his name, which explains his interest in copyright issues.

Other Irish writers, like Geoffrey Keating in the seventeenth century, have similar accounts, even if they do not mention the *cathach* (Keating, 1902–14, Vol. iii, pp. 90–1, Vol. iii, p. 105). They agree with Mánus that Columba returned several times to Ireland, but this is explained by his wearing a veil over his eyes, and having clods of Iona earth attached to his feet, so as not to break his banishment. Mánus also believed a later tradition that Columba was buried at Downpatrick with Saints Patrick and Brigid.

Outside the monastic buildings

There must have been a west range of cloister buildings, where the main entrance now is, but no foundations were found, and this part of the building dates from the 1950s.

Near the west range, the cobbled medieval Street of the Dead ends at a garden planted within the walls of what was once a free-standing stone building, raised over older timber buildings. Excavations indicate that this was a brew house, probably used for baking as well. This work was usually given a separate building to reduce the risk of fire spreading. Beer made from barley was part of the monastic diet. The abbey kitchen probably stood nearby.

Taking the path round the north side of the monastic buildings means passing the abbot's house. Now rebuilt and used as accommodation for abbey guests, this sizeable building was once the place where the abbot could live in some state and entertain important guests.

I should like to have a great ale-feast for the King of Kings; I should like the Heavenly Host to be drinking it for all eternity.

I should like to have the fruits of Faith, of pure devotion; I should like to have the seats of Repentance in my house.

I should like to have the men of Heaven in my own dwelling; I should like the tubs of Long-Suffering to be at their service.

I should like to have the vessels of Charity to dispense; I should like to have the pitchers of Mercy for their company.

I should like there to be Hospitality for their sake; I should like Jesus to be there always.

I should like to have the Three Marys of glorious renown; I should like to have the Heavenly Host from every side.

I should like to be rent-payer to the Lord; he to whom He gives a good blessing has done well in suffering distress.

From tenth- or eleventh-century poem (Jackson, 1971, p. 284)

The building beside this was the reredorter, the latrines, connected to the upper floor of the north range of cloister buildings, where the monks slept. Underneath are remains of the medieval drain, which was flushed by water channelled from the mill-stream.

In the field across the mill-stream are the ruins of the seventeenth-century Bishop's House. This was built at the time of the attempt to make the abbey the cathedral church of the Isles. The

---

This Hebridean folk charm was collected by Alexander Carmichael in the late nineteenth century, and translated by him.

Spell of the Counteracting

I will pluck the gracious yarrow
That Christ plucked with His one hand.

The High King of the Angels
Came with His love and His countenance above me.

Jesus Christ came hitherward
With milk, with substance, with produce,
With female calves, with milk product.

On small eye, on large eye,
Over Christ's property.

In name of the Being of life
Supply me with Thy grace,
The crown of the King of the Angels,
To put milk in udder and gland,
With female calves, with progeny.

May you have the length of seven years
Without loss of calf, without loss of milk,
Without loss of means or of dear friends.

(Carmichael, 1928, Vol. ii, pp. 70–1)

---

house would have been reached by an extension of the road that came to the east end of the abbey.

On the abbey side of the mill-stream but close to this water-course is the building called the infirmary. This had practically disappeared and was rebuilt from its foundations by the Iona Community in the 1960s.

Sick and aged monks would have been housed and nursed here. There may have been a small kitchen inside it, which would have helped to keep the building warm.

The duty of hospitality and spiritual care meant providing for the needs of islanders and pilgrims as well as the community. A monastic library would include medical treatises, especially here on Iona, for Saint Columba had a reputation as a healer.

Treatment would have consisted mainly of giving herbal remedies, and perhaps bone-setting, accompanied by special prayers. In the earlier Middle Ages, until the clergy were banned from performing surgery, simple operations, including removing cataracts, may have been performed here.

The building is now used as a museum, and houses many of the island's carved stones.

The carved stones

These include stones from the early Christian period, many of them taken from the Reilig Oran burial ground and brought in to preserve them. Some are adorned with crosses, some of them ring-headed; and some stones are carved with ornate interlace. Some show signs of reuse. There are names on a few of them, Gaelic and also Norse names in the Scandinavian runic alphabet, a reminder that the history of this place is complex. Some of the Vikings and their descendants are buried here as Christians.

Here are also the broken free-standing high crosses. The raised Saint John's cross (p. 35) and the shaft of Saint Matthew's cross (pp. 51–2) were joined in 2013 by the Saint Oran cross (pp. 36–8), raised again after centuries of lying flat. There are parts too of other crosses.

Most of the immediate impact on the eye comes from the carvings, many in high relief of West Highland figures, the majority dressed as warriors. These come from a later phase of West Highland carvings, and these graveslabs commemorate members of the ruling houses, in particular the Lords of the Isles.

The Michael chapel

Near the infirmary and behind the abbey is another free-standing building known as the Michael chapel. It was probably first built in the early 1200s, perhaps while the abbey church was being constructed, though like so much on Iona it may be on the site of an older structure. It was given a new east window in the fifteenth century. Unlike the abbey, it is oriented true east and therefore lies at an angle to the larger church. This was heavily ruined by the twentieth century, and was largely rebuilt by the Iona Community, and completed in 1959.

The dedication is to the Archangel Michael and, while it is only recorded in recent times, it is known that there was a Michael chapel somewhere on Iona. This warrior archangel was very popular as a defender against evil. Many high places in Western Europe are dedicated to Michael, or to the angels in general. While Iona has a Hill of the Angels on the west coast, this chapel commemorates the angel here at the heart of the monastery.

The rebuilding was funded largely with money from Africa, especially South Africa, and relates to the Iona Community's opposition to apartheid during those years. It is used in the winter by the Community's resident staff for daily services, and is also used for other smaller liturgies, including Catholic Masses. It is laid out with the furnishings of choirstalls. The cupboard in the east wall is a restored medieval aumbry, which was used for the storing of the sacred elements.

After walking around the medieval abbey, the visitor may wish to revisit the Reilig Oran chapel (pp. 65–8), and then follow the road down towards the nunnery. On the way, at what was once the crossing of footpaths, is the fifteenth-century MacLean's cross.

MacLean's cross

This cross is now at a bend of the modern road, almost halfway between the abbey and the nunnery, close to the walls of the modern fields. Raised in the fifteenth century and called MacLean's cross after the ruling family of the time, it is likely to have served as a stopping point, a place that could be circled while praying.

It is a tall slender cross, with a solid ring head that forms a circle. The east face, visible from the road, is finely carved in an abstract design. The other face also contains abstract designs but the circle contains a large figure of Christ on the cross, a figure that catches the rays of the setting sun.

The figure holds his arms out at right angles, the risen Lord coming towards the onlooker. He is fully clothed in a sleeved garment with a pleated skirt to the knees. This may represent the aristocratic linen garment, the pleating of which was emulated by the outer woollen garment from which the kilt derived.

West face of MacLean's cross.

The original road went straight past this cross, through what are now the gardens of the Columba Hotel and up the field towards Saint Mary's chapel, the final stopping place for pilgrims approaching Saint Columba's shrine.

The modern road towards the nunnery has the later parish church on the right, on a site that is believed to be much older. Below it is the island's former school, now the visitors' centre. On the left is a stone marking the donation of the majority of the island's lands to the National Trust for Scotland.

10

The Augustinian Nunnery

The ruined nunnery lies only 200 metres above the harbour. It lies under the shelter of Cnoc Mór, the big hill, outside the monastic *vallum*, the sacred space of the male monastery, which is about 500 metres to the north-east. This was close enough for priests among the monks to say Masses regularly in the nunnery, as women could not become priests themselves.

The nunnery, which followed the Augustinian Rule, was used for some 350 years, until the Reformation prevented the admission of new members and the existing community died out. The ruins were stabilized in 1875 and again in the early twentieth century. In 1922 they were turned into a garden.

We do not know if there was an earlier Columban nunnery on Iona, as there are no records, and fragments of bone uncovered during excavation were too fragile to be dated. The site for the medieval nunnery may have been chosen because it was already a sacred place, perhaps a burial ground for women, with a church beside it.

There are no records of the founding of the nunnery. Few of the later records, such as charters, survive. We know of it mainly from the ruined buildings. Like many nunneries, this one was dedicated to the Virgin Mary.

It is usually said to have been founded around 1207, shortly after the male Columban monastery changed to Benedictine rule. The seventeenth-century *Book of Clanranald*, which extols Ragnall, son of Somerled, and his descendants, says that he founded the nunnery and that his sister Bethag was a nun. Martin Martin saw the tombstone of the first prioress Behag (Bethoc, sometimes

anglicized as Beatrice), when he visited in about 1698. The founding of the Benedictine abbey is also credited to Ragnall, who
became the foremost figure in the Somerled family after the death
of his father in 1164.

The architecture of the earliest parts of the building suggest that
the nunnery could be slightly older than the Benedictine abbey.

By the late twelfth century two other Columban foundations,
Kells and Durrow, had Augustinian nunneries nearby, and there
appear to have been nuns at Derry as well.

It is possible that this nunnery, which shows Irish architectural influence, was established in the final years of the Columban
monastery, though the absence of sources means that we cannot
be certain. The nunnery must date from after 1164, as it is not
mentioned in the *Annals of Ulster*, where there is a relatively long
piece on the attempt by Somerled to re-establish Iona as head of the
Columban family of monasteries in that year. But if the nunnery
was set up later that century, possibly even on the remains of an
earlier, early Christian, nunnery, it might help to explain how the
male monastery became a Benedictine foundation a generation or
two later.

The nunnery was always smaller than the abbey and seems to
have been much poorer through most of its life. Its original stonework is elegant and skilfully carved, with no sign of being rushed
or skimped, which gives another reason to suggest tentatively that
it was founded by the Somerled family a generation or so before
the costly and controversial refoundation of the Benedictine abbey.

The north transept of the abbey shows Romanesque features we
associate with the twelfth century, and this style may have been
adopted because it was already in use nearby. However, it may be
that both foundations were designed after 1200 by an architect
fond of the older styles.

Another consideration throughout these years is that between
1189 and 1214 the archbishops in Norway were both Augustin-
ians. They might have supported the founding of the nunnery.

A peaceful place today, and perhaps through most of their
history, the buildings witnessed the last Norwegian raid on Iona

in 1210. The nuns would have been party to the disturbances in the Hebrides in the following years of the 1220s, which led to the abbot of Iona going with the Bishop of Man and the Isles to seek help from the King of Norway.

We do not know why the Rule for Augustinian canonesses was adopted, but another Scottish nunnery at Perth also followed this Rule. We know nothing of the early nuns other than Bethoc: they may have been local women, or members of Scottish aristocratic families; or they may have come from Ireland, where the similar communities could have provided the training in religious life. There is no record of an affiliation to another nunnery, so it may have been an autonomous, self-ruling foundation.

Bethoc was perhaps a widow who had entered religious life late. Coming from a powerful family, she could have been involved in endowing the nunnery, and she would have been used to running a large household. The later prioresses are likely to have come from similarly wealthy Gaelic families. The few finds excavated at the nunnery indicate a level of wealth in the early days. These include a decorated gold band to keep a headdress in place, a form of jewellery more usually associated with secular than religious life, but perhaps an offering that was used on a statue. Four silver spoons were also found when the nunnery was being landscaped into a garden. They were perhaps precious items used to spoon water into the wine at the celebration of the Eucharist, or more mundanely for use in the parlour with honoured guests, and hidden at some hard time.

Bethoc is thought to have been the original owner of the *Iona Psalter*, now in the National Library of Scotland. This is a Latin illuminated copy of the book of Psalms with additional material that shows it was intended for an Augustinian canoness with an interest in Saint Columba and other Iona saints. The name 'Beota', which is possibly Bethoc, has been written by another hand in one margin (*Argyll 4: Iona*, p. 276). The Psalter appears to be southern English work, perhaps made in the Oxford area in about 1200. It would have been a cherished item in the nuns' community, rather than something used on an everyday basis.

Every evening at Vespers, the *Magnificat*, the Song of Mary from Luke's Gospel, was sung:

My soul glorifies the Lord,
my spirit rejoices in God my Saviour.
He looks on his servant in her lowliness
henceforth all ages will call me blessed.

The Almighty works marvels for me.
Holy God's name!
God's mercy is from age to age,
on those who fear him.

God puts forth his arm in strength
and scatters the proud-hearted.
He casts the mighty from their thrones
and raises the lowly.

He fills the starving with good things,
sends the rich away empty.

He protects Israel his servant,
remembering his mercy,
the mercy promised to our forebears,
to Abraham and his seed forever.

(Grail translation, inclusive version)

The nunnery was partly rebuilt in the fifteenth century when the cloister and its central garden was expanded. After the Reformation it fell into disuse, though part of it was used for sheltering cattle.

The nunnery buildings are an attractive mix, mainly of pink granite in the upper courses, with dark-grey stone in the lower. Both of these would have been available on the island. The dressed stone for carving is a yellow-green sandstone, which has weathered, leaving most of the early carvings hard to decipher. Flagstones seem to have been used to make the roofing material.

Opening page from
Iona Psalter.

The church

This was an imposing structure, with a high arched roof, the last part of which fell in 1822–23. From the outside, a decorative string course appears high on the walls, just under the upper windows, following the lein of the north aisle roof, and rises to embrace the lost east window at one end and the rounded west window at the other.

Like the abbey church, the inner walls would have been painted with decorative features and images of the saints. Statues would also have been used as aids to devotion.

There is a north aisle with a single sloping roof, like that of the abbey's south aisle, divided from the body of the church by elegant rounded arches. These arches were later blocked up and a small door made through one of them.

The side aisle ends with a small chapel at the east end. This chapel was part of the original building, and while it has been restored, it is the only part of the building now roofed. The small east window is in an Irish style with a pointed hood. It is very similar to the window in the choir aisle of the abbey church, part of the extension of about 1220. Here it was already built when the vaulted roof was added. Carried by four crossed arches which were too low to rise above the top of the window, the vaulting meant that part of it became obscured from the inside.

There are still some carvings to be seen in what was once a very fine small chapel. At least one prominent person was buried here, as the gravestone indicates. In the south wall is an aumbry, a small cupboard where the Sacrament was kept, and in the north wall there is a *piscina*, where the vessels were washed after the Communion. This chapel may have been dedicated to the Virgin Mary or been used for small private services, perhaps by some of the many visitors. Above, there is a small room, which is not accessible. It may once have served as a vestry, a place where the vestments and sacred vessels for the services were kept, and where the priests could robe.

The rest of the aisle was cut off from the main body of the church during the changes in the fifteenth century when the arches were blocked. Even so, and in spite of having been open to the wind and rain for so long, some of the carvings at the top of the pillars can still be seen. It looks like two small chapels were made in this part of the church at that time. There was once a west door to the aisle, through which visitors entered.

The main body of the church has a large nave and a chancel. There was an arch between them which rose to a delicate point. The stone springs can still be seen on each side, and there are the remains of some carved faces. In the choir there are also the remains of some of the north wall plaster, though the paintings are long gone.

The choir area was reserved for the choir nuns and the eastern-most area for the presiding priest at the Eucharist, while laysisters and visitors stood in the nave.

The base of the east window comprised of two slender lights can be seen, below which is the base of the high altar. These main windows would have once been filled with expensive glass, per-haps coloured. At the other end of the church is a graceful west window, similar in style to the blocked internal arches. Above this is another, small window, similar to those along the east and west walls.

Remains of arch between nave and chancel.

The church was sketched in 1822, just before the chancel arch and the remaining vaulting collapsed. The chancel arch and the east window are shown, and so is a similar high, two-light window, which let in more light to the altar area and faced south into the cloister area. The base of this can be seen, and near to it has been placed part of another *piscina*.

There were two other high, narrow windows with rounded heads on the southern, cloister, side. Above them, as on the north wall, were more windows, which as at the abbey are in the spaces between the arches. The decorative string course continued round the church and rose up to circle the windows.

The windows at the higher, clerestory, level, though perhaps filled with opaque material, such as thinly stretched animal skin, would have added to the light in this beautifully proportioned and once gracefully decorated church. There was also a floor of sandstone slabs, which probably came from Mull. Parts can be seen in the chancel, which was raised a little higher than the nave, allowing the congregation to view the altar area.

The doorway to the cloisters may have echoed the large windows with narrow lights, because it is exceptionally high and narrow. The entrance and view would have been further narrowed by the wooden door, which swung on a pole that fitted into sockets, one of which can still be seen at the base.

Through it the nuns once processed in and out, day and night, to the private areas of their home. Like the monks, the nuns woke at midnight and descended from the dormitory and into the abbey church to sing the Night Office, Nocturns (Lauds and Matins). They then returned by the same way to sleep. Then followed the other monastic offices: Prime at the start of the day, Nones at about 9 am, Terce at midday, Sext at about 3 pm, Vespers at about 6 pm, and the final office of Compline before they went to bed.

As they processed, they passed by the tombs of their predecessors. One was that of the early sixteenth-century prioress Anna MacLean. The stone was badly damaged when the remaining roof of the chancel fell in. The surviving half, which shows the prioress in her nun's garb, is now under cover, together with many of the other stones.

Nunnery church with arches to side chapel.

At the end of the church, on the south side, are corbels, the projecting stones that carried the roof of a west gallery, which was installed in the fifteenth century when the aisle was blocked off. The carvings may have been moved from their intended sequence, but they give an idea of how different aspects of the church brought to mind the incarnation and redemption. Above the door, the one furthest east has a scene where the angel Gabriel kneels to Mary, who has her hands joined. This is the annunciation, her acceptance of the invitation to be the mother of Jesus. The next corbel has a circular ornamented pattern, perhaps a rosette, a sign sometimes used to represent virginity. Then an angel holds out a scroll, singing with joy at the birth of Jesus. The next figure appears to be a bird, with foliage on each side of its

The nuns, like the monks, structured their day around seven offices, at which the psalms were sung in Latin. There were also daily Masses and other additions to worship, especially on the days of major, or local, saints.

Psalm 8

How great is your name, O Lord our God,
through all the earth!

Your majesty is praised above the heavens;
on the lips of children and of babes
you have found praise to foil your enemy,
to silence the foe and the rebel.

When I see the heavens, the work of your hands,
the moon and the stars which you arranged,
what are we that you should keep us in mind,
mere mortals that you care for us?

Yet you have made us little less than gods;
and crowned us with glory and honour,
you gave us power over the work of your hands,
put all things under our feet.

All of them, sheep and cattle,
yes, even the savage beasts,
birds of the air and fish
that make their way through the waters.

How great is your name, O Lord our God,
Through all the earth!

(Grail translation)

head, perhaps oak leaves, the sign of a mason from Derry. This may be a reference to the descent of the Spirit as a dove at the baptism of Jesus. The last has a worn male face with a crown of thorns. The drama of salvation is presented, close to the doorway which was already old when the corbels were first placed here. As the nuns left the church to go about their work, they brought the drama into their daily lives.

The cloisters

These lie on the warmer south side of the church, as is normal. This private place was where the nuns walked, reflected, prayed, and worked. As in the abbey, a square open arcade opened onto a central garden. The pillars that held up this arcade held carvings, and a few fragments remain.

The central garden may have had flowers grown for pleasure but this sheltered space would have been ideal to grow the herbs used for medicine and also to flavour cooking. An eighteenth-century visitors' account notes that herbs from the old monastic gardens grew wild on the island.

On the east side of the cloisters there were three rooms. The nuns probably slept above. The room nearest the church may have been the parlour, the 'place of speaking', where the nuns could receive guests and do business with the outside world.

The central room, with stone benches around its sides, was the chapter house, the place of daily meetings at which a part of the Rule was read and the business of the community transacted. While it was the duty of choir nuns to attend, and laysisters or novices may have been here at times, the size suggests that the community was always smaller than the male community nearby. The room may have been finely carved, like the abbey chapter house, and the mortared inner walls are likely to have been decorated.

There is not a detailed Augustinian Rule like that of Saint Benedict kept by the monks of the abbey, but various documents, especially a letter from Saint Augustine to a community of nuns

Doorway from cloister to church.

in Hippo in 423, formed the basis of a life lived together in concord and charity. Regular hours of prayer together, fasting, the wearing of the habit, and work to maintain themselves, all formed part of the nuns' daily life. They took oaths of poverty, chastity and obedience to a superior.

South of the chapter house, and closer to the modern road, is another room, perhaps used for storage. At the corner there is another room with the remains of a chimney. This is likely to have been either the kitchen or the warming room, the only parts of the buildings that were heated. The warming room is where nuns went for a short period of relaxation before the final service of the day, Compline, after which the Great Silence started and they went to bed.

The refectory

The large room on the south side of the cloisters appears to have originally been open to a high ceiling (though later, after the Reformation, an extra floor was added to allow accommodation). Here the community ate together while listening to readings from the Lives of the Saints and similar religious writings. This part of the nunnery shows evidence of the rebuilding during the fifteenth century, perhaps like the abbey under the Ua Brolacháin family, or other stonemasons.

Above the middle window on the outside is a worn sheela-na-gig, a carving of a grotesque and aggressive naked female figure sometimes found on church buildings. They are thought to have been placed there to scare away evil spirits (Power, 2012). This figure now looks onto the modern road, but in the Middle Ages faced the nunnery gardens and orchards.

Cloister garth and church.

The Best and Worst Nail in the Ark

The shipwright who made the Ark left empty a place for a nail in it, because he was sure that he himself would not be taken into it. When Noah went into the Ark with his children, as the angel had told him, Noah shut the windows of the Ark and raised his hand to bless it. Now the Devil had come into the Ark along with him as he went into it, and when Noah blessed the Ark the Devil found no other way but the empty hole which the shipwright had left unclosed, and he went into it in the form of a snake; and because of the tightness of the hole he could not go out nor come back, and he was like this until the Flood ebbed; and that is the best and worst nail that was in the Ark.

Irish, sixteenth century (Jackson, 1971, p. 304)

Most of the buildings of the west range have disappeared, and the modern road, laid in the nineteenth century, cuts right through them. In earlier times, the main route passed east of the nunnery and met up with what is now the surfaced road near the place where the National Trust donation slab is.

A smaller pathway passed close to the vanished west range, and then north under the hill. It seems likely that the nuns had a pilgrims' hospice to provide accommodation for women visitors to the island, and this may have occupied the west range. This hospice would have provided them with some income from donations, though not as much as that received by the abbey where the priests could say Masses for the souls of living and dead.

Saint Ronan's chapel

This small, plain, oblong church to the north of the nunnery church was built in the thirteenth century on the site of an earlier church and even earlier burials. It may have been the parish church for the islanders, built small as such churches were and later replaced by something larger to allow more people to stand within during the liturgy. Unusually the door is on the cold north side, which was perhaps intended to ensure the nunnery's privacy. The chapel, now reroofed, is used to display some of the carvings related to the nunnery.

The following story is found in Irish of the fourteenth or fifteenth century and concerns the great monastery of Clonmacnoise on the crossing of the River Shannon in central Ireland. Very similar, and also set at Clonmacnoise, is the account told in Old Norwegian in the thirteenth-century book *The King's Mirror*.

The Air Ship

One day the monks at Clonmacnoise were holding a meeting on the floor of their church, and as they were at their deliberations there they saw a ship sailing over them in the air, going as if it were on the sea. When the crew of the ship saw the meeting and the inhabited place below them, they dropped anchor, and the anchor came right down to the floor of the church, and the priests seized it. A man came down out of the ship after the anchor, and he was swimming as if he were in the water, till he reached the anchor; and they were dragging him down then. 'For God's sake let me go!' said he, 'for you are drowning me.' Then he left them, swimming in the air as before, taking his anchor with him.

(Jackson, 1971, p. 165)

Around the outside

Following the path through the nunnery area, directly to the east of the ruins, there is a series of carved tombstones laid on the grass, pointing eastwards. In Christian burials the head is laid west, so on the last day the dead will rise, their faces towards Jerusalem. The nuns' cemetery stood here, and after the Reformation this site became the islanders' burial ground for women and small children.

To the north of Saint Ronan's chapel lie a number of huge stone bases for free-standing crosses. Some may have been deposited here later, but some may have held early Christian crosses related to the church that stood where Saint Ronan's chapel is now. Other crosses may have been raised at the time of the medieval nunnery.

The lifestyle

The domestic work of the house, including the provision for pilgrims, must have taken up much time. But the main duty of the choir nuns was to sing in the church.

While much of the liturgy was learnt by heart, some of the nuns would have been literate, a skill needed for keeping the lesser-known services, such as those on feast days; and in order to read to the community in the chapter house and refectory. Knowledge was also useful for administrative purposes as the nunnery-owned lands, had tenants and rents were paid. Some nuns may have had medical skills, and reading texts would have benefited them. It is not known how many engaged in writing, for administrative purposes or in order to make a living by copying manuscripts.

Lands that had at some stage come to the nunnery's ownership required managing. The nuns owned the southern part of Iona. Staonaig and the valley that looks south to Columba's Bay appear to have been quite fertile, and the upland was suitable for sheep grazing. There is a record of a prioress visiting nunnery lands in Tiree in the fourteenth century. This windy but 'low-lying island of barley', as the name was later interpreted, has good soils and can be seen most days on the horizon west of Iona. The nunnery

The fourteenth-century *Inchcolm Antiphoner* gives some idea of other forms of musical chant used by communities that took their vision from Saint Columba. Inchcolm, the Isle of Columba, is in the Forth Estuary in eastern Scotland, near Edinburgh and was the home of an early Christian monastery followed by a monastery of Augustinian canons. The surviving fragments of this manuscript contain hymns dedicated to Saint Columba, such as that on page 81. Hymns of this kind in Latin continued to be made and used to praise the founder and protecting patron saint, Columba.

While we cannot know that it was used in the nunnery on Iona, it gives some indication of the additional liturgical material of the time, the kind of thing that would have been sung.

O Columba, our glorious leader,
cleanse our minds, lest the noxious deceiver
harm your servants by the seas' danger,
that around you they may gladly sing.
For you, above all others, it is right that you should hear
voices raised in joy. To this place bend your ear,
That around you may they gladly sing.

(Márkus, in Clancy, 1998, p. 319)

had land too on Coll, and on Benbecula and the Uists in the Outer Hebrides. They also owned the low-lying islands of Heiskeir, also known as the Monach Islands, west of North Uist. This group of now-abandoned islands seem to have been larger in the Middle Ages, and supported a nunnery.

Records are patchy, as often occurs with women's houses, which were usually poorer and less regarded than the men's. The nunnery was largely dependent on the good will of the male community, and fell into disrepute by the fifteenth century through disputes with the monastery.

The following story was first printed well after the Reformation, in 1634 by the Irish priest and historian Geoffrey Keating, but is truly medieval in tone.

Mo Chua's Riches

... Mo Chua and Colum Cille were contemporaries. And when Mo Chua ... was in a hermitage of the wilderness, he had no worldly wealth but a cock and a mouse and a fly. The work the cock used to do for him was to keep matins at midnight. Now the mouse, it would not allow him to sleep more than five hours in a day and a night; and when he wished to sleep longer, being tired from much cross-vigil and prostration, the mouse would begin nibbling his ear, and so awoke him. Then the fly, the work it did was to walk along every line he read in his psalter, and when he rested from singing his psalms the fly would stay on the line he had left until he returned again to read his psalms. It happened soon after this that these three treasures died; and Mo Chua wrote a letter afterwards to Colum Cille when he was in Iona in Scotland, and complained of the death of this flock. Colum Cille wrote to him, and this is what he said: 'Brother,' said he, 'you must not wonder at the death of the flock that has gone from you, for misfortune never comes but where there are riches ...'

(Jackson, 1971, pp. 297–8)

This story is one of the many humorous stories circulated about Saint Columba. It looks back to his time, when penitential practices included cross vigils, praying with the arms extended in a cross; prostrations and multiple genuflections; and cutting down on sleep. The 'flock' refers to the hermit Mo Chua having no other monastic following.

The laysisters would have undertaken the bulk of heavy domestic work, including farming, gardening, milking, butter- and cheese-making, preserving food, foraging for plants in season to vary the diet, scouring the shoreline for shellfish and seaweeds, haymaking, and perhaps working with leather. There are likely to have been local men employed to do the more distant work, like shepherding and perhaps shearing.

Milking and milk-processing was women's work, and the practice of transhumance was followed. While cattle were taken to other pastures during the summer months, the home field was hayed to ensure winter fodder. Mowing hay was usually man's work, as the cutting uses the upper body muscles, but raking and turning the mown grass, and stacking it when dried, were usually women's tasks. Similarly, at harvest-time men usually cut the crops, while women stacked and gleaned.

The food was probably much like that in the earlier Columban period. A record of the fourteenth-century abbey notes wheat, barley, and white and black 'pin-head' oats. These needed to be harvested in season, then threshed, dried in a corn kiln, and the corn ground for meal. Straw was used for bedding and is later known for thatching. Ale was made from barley, so the brewing process would have been one of the chores to be done at the nunnery. Fine wheat was probably kept for feast days, and the best of the flour for the Communion breads. Imported wine was also used for Communion, and perhaps also drunk on feast days.

The diet was supplemented by berries in season, seafood and very probably also marine mammals such as seal. Wild birds such as geese were eaten, as were eggs. Puffin and fulmar are known to have been prized later for their oil, used as fuel and lighting.

There was at times meat, especially at the autumn slaughter-time or at festivals. All parts of the animals were used, including the marrow from the bones. The nuns may well have kept domestic fowl, hens and geese, for eggs and meat and feathers for bedding.

While agricultural improvements came over the centuries, assisted by communications among monastic communities and knowledge about developments on the Continent, food was seasonal and the diet was probably monotonous. In the Middle Ages, records from tenants indicate that wheat and barley were used to pay rental, as was cheese in some places.

Clothing was made from wool and linen, and the production was usually regarded as female work. After shearing, sheep's wool had to be cleaned and teased, then carded ready for spinning. This was done by hand, by drop-spinning, a laborious business which many women learnt to do while walking about doing other things. The spinning had to be even in quality to make good cloth. The spun yarn retained its natural colours of creamy-white, brown, black and grey. While the nuns were expected to dress in simple style, some of the wool might be dyed, before or after weaving, especially if the cloth was to be sold. Dying required the gathering of plants or seashells, and then creating a dye bath.

Weaving was also laborious, done on upright frames. The cloth then had to be fulled, beaten, usually with stale urine as an agent, to thicken the cloth and make it windproof.

Linen clothing also involved several processes. The flax plants had to be grown, harvested, and the stems left to ret in water, allowing the outer parts to rot. The inner fibres were collected after this smelly process had finished, and were dried, scutched (beaten), and finally spun while damp, then woven, and bleached by laying the fabric out on dry moonlit nights.

Fine materials were used as church furnishings, often with embroidered or other decorative edges. Some nuns may have made liturgical garments out of fine linen and imported silks. These long-perished items may have been of high quality.

Most fabric was used for clothing, which had to be cut out and sewn. Clothing was an investment of time, skill and energy, so cut-offs were retained, and used for small items, or for patching, as clothes were used until they fell apart, sometimes passed on to the poor when they became old, or else used as underwear. During the Middle Ages, knitting arrived from the south. This was less wasteful of wool for some clothing, but was less windproof.

Good clothing was a sign of status and dignity, even among these women who had relinquished fine costume on entering the nunnery.

Footwear, like other essentials such as ropes and harness for horses, produced from tanned leather had to be made or bought from others.

The Benedictine monastery owned rights to limestone, ideal for building and also used for the lime baths required to make vellum and parchment for writing, from calf- and lamb-skins. It also had rights to an exposed coal seam on Mull, which provided a good source of fuel. Wood, including driftwood, and turf, peat, were more regular sources for cooking and heating. The nuns may have had similar rights.

Nunnery church west window.

Though the community must have suffered as did all communities by the rapid decrease in population caused by the Black Death, the nunnery building was expanded in the fifteenth century, a time of piety. This suggests that it had enough revenues, or received endowments from wealthy benefactors to allow the work to be done.

Pilgrims kept coming to Iona, and needed hospitality. The ruins and garden today speak of the long history of spiritual engagement.

The *Aberdeen Breviary* of 1510 contains a hymn to Saint Columba from the end of the medieval period. Like the Inchcolm manuscript, we can gain from it an understanding of how the monks of the Benedictine monastery may have conducted the liturgies. Presumably, something similar happened at the nunnery, where the services paralleled those of the abbey.

> Let us joyfully celebrate the great feast of Columba, happy in this night season, with musical prayer.
> He was born of royal stock, pure was his childhood, he despised earthly glory, desiring only things of heaven.
> He had worked great marvels, had cured all diseases, had foretold the future, had given life to the dead;
> He had assuaged enemies and wars, had seen the citizens of heaven; the good that he had spoken in words, he fulfilled himself by his deeds.
> He had been head over all the people of the Isles; for seven years he had been king, he had dispensed laws, he had stood as both king and teacher.
> Accept our prayers, father Columba, most holy of monks; protect and guide us in the way of peace.

From the *Aberdeen Breviary* (Macquarrie, 2000, pp. 28–9)

PART THREE

Afterword

We see Iona in the twenty-first century through the many changes that have come since the Reformation. This section briefly covers the intervening centuries, and then considers places on the island visited for their significance to past and present people.

Iona since the Reformation

The Protestant Reformation of the mid-sixteenth century led to the end, as happened elsewhere in Scotland, of both monastery and nunnery on Iona. New entrants to the religious life were not permitted, and existing monks and nuns were pensioned off, but allowed to live out their days in their monastic homes.

The premises were too large and too far from the centre of Scots power in the east of the country to mean they had much use to the religious or secular authorities. In the 1630s there was an attempt to reinstate the abbey as the cathedral of the Isles, and the Bishop's House was built in the land across the mill-stream north of the abbey. This attempt was short-lived, and the church itself was in such poor condition in the 1640s that King Charles I agreed to send money towards its restoration. The Civil War intervened, and nothing more is heard until 1688 when the visiting William Sachaverell noted that the islanders were still using the church for Sunday worship.

Ten years later, the Hebridean Martin Martin visited and made notes on the state of the buildings and lifestyle of the islanders. The roof of the abbey church fell in during the early eighteenth century. From the mid-eighteenth century onwards, there came a succession of visitors, many of them religious tourists, who found that the picturesque ruins raised their minds to lofty thoughts and their imaginations to speculate on the grandeur of the past. The Reilig Oran cemetery with its many mortuary stones was a major focus. Accounts by local guides, and by guidebooks written by these visitors, ensured that the stones were regarded as marking the resting places of the kings of Scotland, Ireland and Norway, though most were those of the family of the Lords of the Isles and their immediate predecessors.

More pragmatically, the islanders made a living from farming and fishing, supplemented by tourism. They used some buildings for livestock accommodation, and loose stones were used in building new structures. Stories were recounted about Columba and the real or imagined past to the religious visitors who came looking for such fulfilment of their expectations. The visitors included Dr Samuel Johnson and James Boswell in the late eighteenth century (Johnson complained that cattle were kept in the nuns' church). In the nineteenth century a youthful and sick Felix Mendelssohn came, and also famously went to Fingal's Cave. Other visitors included Queen Victoria and Prince Albert; and many less well-known people.

The roof of the nunnery church chancel collapsed in the early nineteenth century. From 1828 onwards, the islanders had their own parish church. The island minister had only been installed in the church and manse for a few years when he felt compelled to leave during the 'Great Disruption' of 1843 when members of the Church of Scotland broke away to form the Free Presbyterian Church. A Free Church congregation formed and initially met outdoors in the Reilig Oran, but in time built the chapel at Martyrs' Bay, which is now a private house.

Towards the end of the nineteenth century, a group of artists, many of them influenced by the Celtic Revival movement, visited regularly. These rather bohemian summer residents were supplemented by the day trippers who now came by steamship. Indeed, as travel became cheaper, more religious visitors came, and Bishop's

House, the Episcopalian retreat house was built. Finally, after the ruins were gifted to Trustees, work began on rebuilding the abbey church. The nunnery became a garden in 1922.

This medieval poem was attributed to Saint Columba, and became popular when recast as a hymn in the late nineteenth century.

I walk the lonely mountain road –
my King of Suns – and darkest glen,
no nearer death, though I be alone
than fared I with three thousand men.

Though fared I forth three thousand strong
all lusty lads with bodies tough,
and mighty death came stalking me,
would they ward him off, were they enough?

If one be fey there's no safe place
and seeking sanctuary is vain,
while seems to me scarce natural
a path whereon the undoomed are slain.

A man may think to take my life,
appropriate my purse and pence,
but till the fair Lord gives assent
he'll plot and plan and I'll not hence.

Where today stands any man
with power to snatch my life away?
None but the Maker of earth and sky,
The Shaper of the summer-day.

Signs do not stop me setting out
– Did someone sneeze? – for my last breath
will be when foot compulsively
treads the awaiting sod of death.

I fear no more to walk alone;
let world, which shaped me, gave me birth,
take not untimely back but wait
for nut-ripe falling to the earth ...

And why this seeking company?
Is it perhaps that you
are set on scaring death away
in awe of a great retinue?

Indeed, indeed, avoiding death
takes too much time and too much care,
and then, at the end of all,
he catches each one unaware.

May nine ranks of angels and my God
be ever watchful over me,
from terror, from caverns of white death
protecting, bearing company.

Eleventh or twelfth century (Carney, 1985, pp. 42–7)

In the late nineteenth century, Celtic Studies was developing as an academic discipline, and the products of its scholarship were relatively accessible to the general reader through the production of editions and poetic translations on which artists and poets modelled their own work.

The Celtic Revival brought a whole new way of seeing Iona through the painters who looked for atmosphere, and also through a movement that saw its sources in the past and among the people. It relished the folk tradition as it was known, mainly through the translations of the collector Alexander Carmichael. His material was adapted and emulated, while much of the more Catholic and 'rustic' material was silently discarded. The emulators sought to retain Carmichael's English style, which was of its time and through which he attempted to convey something of the poetic construction of his oral Gaelic sources. The writer William Sharp, known under his pen-name as Fiona MacLeod, used this style for his poetry and prose. He was a regular visitor, while the silver-smiths Alexander and Euphemia Ritchey copied their designs from the cross slabs and other carvings on the island.

The following comes from a longer poem by Fiona MacLeod (William Sharp, 1860–1905), which he treats as a translation from Gaelic. These lines were taken and adapted, probably by a member of the Iona Community in the middle of the twentieth century, to form this well-known prayer.

Deep peace of the running wave to you.
Deep peace of the flowing air to you.
Deep peace of the quiet earth to you.
Deep peace of the shining stars to you.
Deep peace of the Son of Peace to you.

The idea of rebuilding the remainder of the abbey had been mooted for some time, but it was in 1937 that a Church of Scotland minister, George MacLeod, began the rebuilding along with some followers. MacLeod was already well known for social activism in Glasgow, and from the start he determined that the work would be led by otherwise unemployed craftsmen, assisted by the unskilled labour of young Church of Scotland clergymen and students. The intention was to work in the summer, disperse to work in impoverished areas in the winter, and finally to use the rebuilt abbey as a training college for clergy. The approach, radical at a time when class boundaries were strong, was controversial on many levels. War intervened and the work stopped but continued afterwards, and was completed in 1967.

Throughout, summer visitors attended 'conferences' on Iona, on topical subjects that sought to address a new world order and to bring freshness to church worship. MacLeod's own blend of mysticism and practical action brought its own attractions. A key development was the provision of good liturgy, and from the start this was accompanied by singing.

From 'A Temple not made with hands', a prayer of
George MacLeod:

We are Your temple not made with hands.
We are Your body.
If every wall should crumble, and every church decay,
we are Your habitation.
Nearer are You than breathing, closer than hands and feet.
Ours are the eyes with which You, in the mystery,
Look out in compassion on the world.

So we bless You for this place.
For Your directing of us, Your redeeming of us,
and Your indwelling.
Take us 'outside the camp', Lord.
Outside holiness.
Out to where soldiers gamble,
and thieves curse,
and nations clash
at the cross-roads of the world ...
So shall this building continue to be justified.

(MacLeod 2007, p. 67)

In the late sixties, when the idea of a clergy training college had been abandoned, and the Community had long been ecumenical, women became full members, rather than as hitherto, auxiliary workers and fundraisers. The centres were and are run by staff and open to weekly guests who use shared bedrooms and facilities, and assist with domestic tasks. Worship remains key to the Community, and the music in particular has been made popular by the hymnwriters and worship leaders John Bell and Graham Maule.

In 2000 the Trustees placed the buildings under the management of the public heritage body Historic Scotland. The Community are their tenants in the abbey, and own other properties on the island, including the purpose-built MacLeod Centre.

The Iona Community today has some 270 members, plus many more associates and friends. The Community remains dispersed and ecumenical, meeting in local groups and in regular plenary sessions. Members live by a Rule which includes daily prayer and Bible study; action for justice and peace, usually undertaken near to where the individual member lives; accounting for the use of time, money and the environment; and meeting and accounting to each other. Members are prayed for by rota in the abbey services.

Iona's other sites

The two strands at the north end of the island are much visited for their sandy dunes and the clear waters. There are offshore craggy islets. Beyond, can be seen the islands of Staffa, Dutchman's Cap, and on the horizon the low-lying Tiree, the island of barley, which had many connections with Iona's abbey, and later the nunnery. By tradition, the now peaceful North Strand is where the Vikings beached their longboats and set off to raid the island.

The North Strand.

Many of the other places can be visited in company on the Community's weekly pilgrim walk. This starts from Saint Martin's cross at 10.15 am on Tuesdays, and ends at about 4 pm. Like a shorter on-road walk, it is free to all-comers.

Many of the sites can also be seen from the sea, on a boat journey round the island.

Martyrs' Bay to the south of the village was one of the island landing places into the 1940s, and is thought to be the place where the dead were brought to be buried on Iona.

Due to erosion, bones were exposed in the field west of the road, and investigation indicated this was an ancient burial ground.

In more recent times, this bay is where the 'puffers', the coalboats that plied the Hebrides in the late nineteenth and early twentieth centuries, put in. It was used for unloading materials during the rebuilding of the abbey.

There is another bay and then Sandeels' Bay to the south, just after the road turns inland. Sandeels were once part of the fishing economy. Another sign of past livelihoods is the marble quarry, set beside the rocky section of shore, where boats pulled up to load with the stone, which was prized in early times, and in more recent centuries in places far from Iona. The machinery from the last phase of activity is still in place and is maintained by volunteers. The site is now protected by law.

The high altar of the medieval abbey was made of Iona marble.

Over the centuries that the church was in ruins, souvenir hunters took pieces away. The current Communion table is made of the last substantial pieces of marble to be quarried on the island.

Beyond this is Columba's Bay, which is viewed as the place where Columba first stepped ashore on Iona, and was unable to see his native Ireland. The bay is divided by a large central rock which gives the appearance of an upturned keel. The natural pebbles of the beach have been formed into large cairns, the age and purpose of which are not known.

This is the translation by the twentieth-century poet and scholar Helen Waddell (1889–1965) of a section of the *Altus Prosator*, a poem on the creation and redemption, written in Latin on Iona and attributed to Saint Columba.

Day of the king most righteous,
The day is nigh at hand,
The day of wrath and vengeance,
The darkness on the land.

Day of thick clouds and voices,
Of mighty thundering,
A day of narrow anguish
And bitter sorrowing.

The love of women's over,
And ended is desire,
Men's strife with men is quiet,
And the world lusts no more.

Latin (Waddell, 1929, p.79. From *Altus Prosator*, attributed to Saint Columcille. There are modern translations in Carey, 2000, pp. 44–5 and Clancy and Márkus, 1995, pp. 50–1)

The south-west coast of the island is rugged, with inland a small heath on which is the freshwater Loch Staonaig, where the nuns once owned land and where cattle were taken for the summer pastures into the nineteenth century. Until recently it provided the water supply for the island.

To the west is the curving Bay at the Back of the Ocean. The *machair* where the monks once grew grain is now in part a golf course. A ship foundered in this bay in the nineteenth century, and the crew who died are buried in Reilig Oran. Pieces of coal were found washed up until recently. At the north end there is the ancient Dun Bhuirg. The Hill of the Angels overlooks the end of the tarmac road.

Other places visited on pilgrimage are a round stone enclosure called the Hermit's Cell, near what may have been an old path used by the monks to cross the island. Nearby is a walled enclosure beneath overhanging rock. These structures are of indeterminate date but associated in popular imagination with Saint Columba. They may have had a use in later times for animal management.

The highest point on the island, Dún Í, has no 'dun' or fort, but a stone cairn marks it. Many of the surrounding islands can be seen from its height, and below is the ancient site of Columba's abbey.

Preservation, restoration, presentation and stewardship of the island continue. There are ongoing small-scale archaeological investigations, and historical research helps us to understand more of the background to the many phases of life on the island. There remains a resident community of islanders, engaging in crofting, fishing, and activities relating to the centres and to tourism. Stewardship of the spiritual life continues, with regular worship in the abbey, in the parish church, Bishop's House and the Catholic House of Prayer, together with other, often informal events.

Above all, Iona remains a place for private prayer and reflection. For many people, the true heritage is that prayer is ongoing, and many people leave behind something of their spiritual engagement. Without adding to or changing what is visible, there is a rich atmosphere. It is a place of deep conversations and sometimes of life-changing experiences.

This prayer was probably first composed by Arthur Gray Butler (1831–1909). It was used in a prose form by the Scout movement during the 1930s. It became known in the Iona Community and was rewritten several times until it reached its current poetic form.

O Christ, the Master Carpenter
Who at the last through wood and nails
Purchased our whole salvation,
Wield well your tools
In the workshop of your world
So that we who come rough-hewn to your bench
May here be fashioned
To a truer beauty of your hand.
We ask it for your own name's sake. Amen.

References and Further Reading

For the general reader, Adomnán's *Life of Saint Columba* is a good place to start. Sharpe's Introduction and Notes are particularly useful. Bede's *Ecclesiastical History* is a similar and very readable source, written from a Northumbrian perspective. Brown's *How Christianity came to Britain and Ireland* gives an overview of the development of Christianity in both Ireland and Britain.

Sources for both poetry and prose are Jackson's *Celtic Miscellany* and Carey's *King of Mysteries*, while the poetry directly associated with Iona can be found in Clancy and Markús' *Iona*. Clancy's edition *The Triumph Tree* is a compilation of the earliest Scottish poetry in translation. Poems from the Irish tradition can be found in the older publications listed here, and are often printed in Miscellanies, such as Murray's *The Deer's Cry*. MacMurchaidh's bilingual collection covers the early and medieval periods as well as later religious poetry from Ireland.

The historical background is covered extensively in what is known as *Argyll 4: Iona*, the official inventory of the monuments, and more accessibly in the official guides published by Historic Scotland. Herbert's is the standard academic work on early Iona and its Irish links; and it contains a translation of the Middle Irish *Life of Saint Columba* (also called the Old Irish Homily, pp. 248–69). Broun and Clancy's *Spes Scotorum* is a collection of essays that give insight into the literature, traditions and archaeology of Iona. Some of the research papers from a recent conference on Iona in 2012 can be found at www.ionahistory.org.uk/researchconference.

For art, Meehan's 1994 guide to the *Book of Kells*, which is regularly reprinted, is helpful; and his much larger and splendidly illustrated 2012 work provides an update on the scholarship that has helped to unlock the artistry. Simms' short 1988 work, though now dated, remains in print and provides an insight into the spirituality behind the work. The current writer has a book nearing completion on the use of the illuminations as icons. Forthcoming works by the current generation of scholars will help us to understand the book further.

There are numerous books about Iona in recent times, including those by Mairi MacArthur, while practical books on pilgrimage around the modern carvings in the cloisters by Mathers, the abbey by Polhill, and the island by Bentley and Paynter have been produced by Wild Goose Publishing. Books about the Iona Community include those by Ferguson, Shanks, and a chapter in my *Celtic Quest*. The Community's journal *Coracle* has articles about current activities.

Adomnán, 1991, *Life of Saint Columba*, Richard Sharpe, trans. and Introduction, Harmondsworth: Penguin.

Annals of Ulster (to A.D. 1131), 1983, Seán Mac Airt and Gearóid Mac Niocaill, eds and trans., Dublin: Institute of Advanced Studies; *Annala Uladh: Annals of Ulster 1887–1901*, 1998, W. M. Hennessy and Mac Carthy, eds and trans., 4 vols, reprinted with Introduction, Nollaig Ó Muraíle, Dublin: Institute of Advanced Studies. Texts and translations at www.ucc.ie/celt.

Argyll 4, see RCAHMS.

Bede, 1990, *Ecclesiastical History of the English People*, Leo Shirley-Price, trans., rev. ed. R. E. Latham, Harmondsworth: Penguin.

Bentley, Jane and Neil Paynter, 2011, *Around a Thin Place*, Glasgow: Wild Goose Publications.

Broun, Dauvit and Thomas Owen Clancy, eds, 1999, *Spes Scotorum, Hope of Scots: Saint Columba, Iona and Scotland*, Edinburgh: T. and T. Clark.

Brown, Michelle, 2006, *How Christianity Came to Britain and Ireland*, Oxford: Lion.

Carey, John, 2000, *King of Mysteries: Early Irish Religious Writings*, Dublin: Four Courts Press.

Carmichael, Alexander, 1900–71, *Carmina Gadelica*, 6 vols, Edinburgh: Scottish Academic Press. English translations republished 1991, Floris Books: Edinburgh.

Carney, James, 1985, *Medieval Irish Lyrics with The Irish Bardic Poet*, Portlaoise: Dolmen Press.

Carver, Martin, 2008, *Portmahomack: Monastery of the Picts*, Edinburgh: Edinburgh University Press.

Christian, Jessica and Charles Stiller, 2000, *Iona Portrayed: Iona through Artists' Eyes, 1760–1960*, Inverness: The New Iona Press.

Chronica Regum Manniae et Insularum: The Chronicle of Man and the Sudreys, 1874, D. Goss, ed., Douglas: The Manx Society.

Clancy, Thomas Owen and Gilbert Márkus, 1995, *Iona: The Earliest Poetry of a Celtic Monastery*, Edinburgh: Edinburgh University Press.

Clancy, Thomas, ed., 1998, *The Triumph Tree: Scotland's Earliest Poetry, 550–1350*, Edinburgh: Canongate.

Coracle (1938–), The Journal of the Iona Community, Glasgow.

Cowie, Ian, 1995, 'The Archaeologists', *Coracle*, November 1995, p. 20.

Farr, Carol, 1997, *The Book of Kells*, London: British Library.

Ferguson, Ronald, 1988, *Chasing the Wild Goose: The Story of the Iona Community*, 2nd ed., Glasgow: Wild Goose Publishing.

Flower, Robin, 1947, *The Irish Tradition*, Oxford: Clarendon Press.

Goss, D., 1874, *Chronicon regum Manniæ et insularum: The Chronicle of Man and the Sudreys*. With historical notes by P. A. Munch, Douglas: Manx Society.

Greene, David and Frank O'Connor, 1990, *A Golden Treasury of Irish Poetry A.D. 600–1200*, Dingle: Brandon.

Herbert, Máire, 1996, *Iona, Kells and Derry: The History and Hagiography of the Monastic Familia of Columba*, Dublin: Four Courts Press.

Herbert, Máire and Pádraig Ó Riain, eds and trans., 1988, *Betha Adamnán: The Irish Life of Adamnán*, London: Irish Texts Society.

Jackson, Kenneth, 1935, *Studies in Early Celtic Nature Poetry*, Cambridge: Cambridge University Press; (facsimile reprint 1995) Felinfach: Llanerch Publishers.

Jackson, Kenneth, 1971, *A Celtic Miscellany*, 2nd edn, Harmondsworth: Penguin.

Keating, Geoffrey, 1902–14, *Foras Feasa ar Éirinn: the History of Ireland*, 4 vols, Patrick Dinneen, ed., London: Irish Texts Society.

Kelly, Fergus, 1997, *Early Irish Farming: A Study Based Mainly on the Law-Texts of the 7th and 8th Centuries AD*, Dublin: Institute for Advanced Studies.

Lacey, Brian, 1997, *Colum Cille and the Columban Tradition*, Dublin: Four Courts Press.

Lacey, Brian, 2006, *Cenél Conaill and the Donegal Kingdoms AD 500–800*, Dublin: Four Courts Press.

MacArthur, Mairi, 1991, *That Illustrious Island: Iona through Travellers' Eyes*, Iona: New Iona Press.

MacDonald, Janet C., 2010, Iona's Local Associations in Argyll and the Isles, c.1203–c.1575, unpublished PhD, University of Glasgow. Used with permission.

MacLeod, George, 1985, rev. 2007, *The Whole Earth Shall Cry Glory*, Glasgow: Wild Goose Publishing, www.ionabooks.com

MacMurchaidh, Ciarán, ed., *Lón Anama: Poems for Prayer from the Irish Tradition*, Baile Átha Cliath [Dublin]: Bord na Leabhar Gaeilge.

Macquarrie, Alan, 'The Offices for St Columba (9 June) and St Adomnán (23 September) in the Aberdeen Breviary', *Innes Review* 51, 2000, pp. 1–39.

Márkus, Gilbert, 2008, *Adomnán's Law of the Innocents: Cáin Adomnáin*, rev. edn, Kilmartin: Kilmartin House Trust.

Márkus, Gilbert, 2010, '*Adiutor Laborantium*: a poem by Adomnán?', in Wooding et al., eds, *Adomnán of Iona*, pp. 145–61.

Martin, Martin, 1934, *A Description of the Western Isles of Scotland circa 1695*, Stirling: Eneas Mackay.

Mathers, Ewan, 2001, *The Cloisters of Iona Abbey*, Glasgow: Wild Goose Publications.

Meehan, Bernard, 1994, *The Book of Kells* (popular version), London: Thames and Hudson.

Meehan, Bernard, 2012, *The Book of Kells* (authoritative version), London: Thames and Hudson.

Meyer, Kuno, 1911, *Selections of Ancient Irish Poetry*, London: Constable.

Murphy, Gerard, 1956, *Early Irish Lyrics: Eighth to Twelfth Century*, Oxford: Clarendon Press.

Murray, Patrick, ed., 1986, *The Deer's Cry: A Treasury of Irish Religious Verse*, Dublin: Four Courts Press.

Ó Carragáin, Tomás, 2010, *Churches in Early Medieval Ireland*, New Haven/London: Yale University Press.

Ó Corráin, Donnchadh, Liam Breathnach and Kim McCone, eds, 1989, *Sages, Saints and Storytellers: Celtic Studies in Honour of Professor James Carney*, Maynooth: An Sagart.

Ó Corráin, Donnchadh, 1989, 'Early Irish Hermit Poetry', in Ó Corráin, Breathnach and McCone, pp. 251–67.

O'Donnell, Manus [Mánus Ó Domhnaill], 1998, *The Life of Colum Cille*, ed. and trans., Brian Lacey, Dublin: Four Courts Press.

O'Sullivan, Jerry et al., 1994, 'Excavation of an early church and a women's cemetery at St. Ronan's medieval parish church, Iona', *Proceedings of the Society of Antiquaries of Scotland* 124, pp. 327–65.

Polhill, Chris, 2006, *A Pilgrim's Guide to Iona Abbey*, Glasgow: Wild Goose Publications.

Powell, Elinor D. U., 2007, *The High Crosses of Ireland: Inspirations in Stone*, Dublin: Liffey Press.

Power, Rosemary, 2005. 'Meeting in Norway: Norse-Gaelic relations in the Kingdom of Man and the Hebrides', *Saga-Book* 29, pp. 5–66.

Power, Rosemary, 2010, *The Celtic Quest: A Contemporary Spirituality*, Dublin: Columba.

Power, Rosemary, 2012. 'Iona's Sheela-na-gig and Its Visual Context', *Folklore* 123, pp. 330–54.

The Psalms: An Inclusive Language Version Based on the Grail Translation, 1993, London: Harper-Collins.

RCAHMS: The Royal Commission on the Ancient and Historical Monuments of Scotland, 1982, *An Inventory of the Monuments, Vol. 4, Iona*, by Ian Fisher, Edinburgh: RCAHMS.

Ritchie, Anna, 1997, *Iona*, London: B.T. Batsford Ltd/Historic Scotland.

Scott, Nicki, 2012, *Iona Abbey and Nunnery*, Edinburgh: Historic Scotland.

Sharpe, Richard, 2012, 'Iona in 1771: Gaelic tradition and visitors' experience', *Innes Review* 63, pp. 161–259.

Shanks, Norman, 1999, *Iona: God's Energy*, London: SPCK.

Simms, George Otto, 1988, *Exploring the Book of Kells*, Dublin: O'Brien Press.

Stokes, Whitley, 1905, *The Martyrology of Oengus the Culdee*, repr. 1984, London: Henry Bradshaw Society.

Thomas, Charles, 1957, 'Excavations on Iona, 1956 and 1957', *Coracle* 31 (November), pp. 10–14.

Thomas, Charles, 1959, 'The Excavations on Iona During 1958 and 1959', *Coracle* 35 (November), pp. 12–17.

Waddell, Helen, 1929, *Mediæval Latin Lyrics*, Hamondsworth: Penguin.

Williams, N. J. A., 1989, 'Some Irish Plant Names', in Ó Corráin, Breathnach and McCone, pp. 449–62.

Wooding, Jonathan, with Rodney Aist, Thomas Owen Clancy and Thomas O'Loughlin, eds, 2010, *Adomnán of Iona: Theologian, Lawmaker, Peacemaker*, Dublin: Four Courts Press, pp. 145–61.

Acknowledgements of Sources

The author and publisher are grateful for permission to reproduce extracts, including material under copyright, from the following publications. They would welcome any information on omissions or inaccuracies.

Broun, Dauvit and Thomas Owen Clancy, eds, 1999, *Spes Scotorum, Hope of Scots: Saint Columba, Iona and Scotland*, Edinburgh: T. and T. Clark:
Fourteenth-century *Inchcolm Antiphoner* (p. 81).

Carey, John, 2000, *King of Mysteries: Early Irish Religious Writings*, Dublin: Four Courts Press:
Old Irish poem *Aipgitir Chrábaid*, 'Alphabet of Devotion', attributed to the nephew of Columcille, Colmán (pp. 30–1). Reproduced by permission of the author, John Carey.

Carmichael, Alexander, 1900–71, *Carmina Gadelica*, 6 vols, Edinburgh: Scottish Academic Press. English translations republished 1991, Floris Books: Edinburgh:
Hebridean folk charm (p. 104).

Carney, James, 1985, *Medieval Irish Lyrics with The Irish Bardic Poet*, Portlaoise: Dolmen Press:
Poem attributed to Adomnán, *Life of Saint Columba* (p. 18).
Eleventh-century Irish poem (pp. 53–4).
Medieval poem attributed to Saint Columba (pp. 133–4).

Clancy, Thomas, ed., 1998, *The Triumph Tree: Scotland's Earliest Poetry, 550–1350*, Edinburgh: Canongate:
Twelfth-century prayer in Latin on a Life of Saint Columba (p.62).
Fourteenth-century *Inchcolm Antiphoner* (pp. 81 & 125).

Clancy, Thomas Owen and Gilbert Márkus, 1995, *Iona: The Earliest Poetry of a Celtic Monastery*, Edinburgh: Edinburgh University Press:
Cantemus in omni die (p. 46).
Adiutor Laborantium (pp. 21–2).
Noli Pater (p. 10).
Máire Herbert and Padraig Ó Riain, 1988, poem attributed to Adomnán, *Life of Saint Columba* (p. 28).

Flower, Robin, 1947, *The Irish Tradition*, Oxford: Clarendon Press:
Eighth–tenth century Irish poem (p. 38).

Jackson, Kenneth, 1935, *Studies in Early Celtic nature Poetry*, Cambridge: Cambridge University Press; (facsimile reprint 1995) Felinfach: Llanerch Publishers:
Tenth-century Irish poem (p. 47).
Twelfth-century Irish poem (pp. 68–9).

Jackson, Kenneth, 1971, *A Celtic Miscellany*, 2nd edn, Harmondsworth: Penguin:
Brendan Kennelly, fifteenth-century Irish poem by Tadghd Óg Ó hUiginn, in Murray, 1986, *The Deer's Cry* (p. 92).
Tenth–eleventh-century poem (p. 103).

MacLeod, Fiona (pseudonym of William Sharp, 1860–1905), A Gaelic blessing, probably adapted by members of the Iona Community in the mid-twentieth century (p. 135).

MacLeod, George Fielden, 'A Temple Not Made with Hands', in *The Whole Earth Shall Cry Glory*, 2007, Glasgow: Wild Goose Publications (see www.ionabooks.com) (p. 136).

Macquarrie, Alan, 'The Offices for St Columba (9 June) and St Adomnán (23 September) in the Aberdeen Breviary', *Innes Review* 51, 2000, pp. 1–39: Sixteenth-century hymn to Saint Columba from the *Aberdeen Breviary* (p. 130).

Meyer, Kuno, 1911, *Selections of Ancient Irish Poetry*, London: Constable: Eighth–ninth century Irish poem (p. 12).